Monetary Economics and the Performance
of the Banking Sector in Sudan

Professor Issam AW Mohamed

DEDICATION

I dedicate my words and writings to my late Great father Abdel Wahab Bob the Lawyer who spent his life defending the weak and the meek people of Sudan.

God almighty in the holy Koran said: God does not change the people unless they changed themselves

So when shall we do

DEDICATION

I dedicate my words and writings to my late Great father
Abdel Wahab Bob the Lawyer who spent his life
defending the weak and the meek people of Sudan.

God almighty in the holy Koran said: God does not
change the people unless they changed themselves

So when shall we do

1. Table of Contents

Monetary Economics and the Performance of the Banking Sector in Sudan

Professor Issam A.W. Mohamed

2. Abstract

Currently, Sudan is living under abnormal economic conditions, which can be described as suffocating. The banking sector has been suffering from the problem of cash outflow over the last three decades, generating the following impacts: Loss of banking sector of its role of financial intermediation, cash scarcity in the banking sector, large government borrowings from unreal source of finance, thus, more inflation. Rumors are that government lost control of the economic situation, reverted to printing money to cater for lack of liquidity. Truly, bad economic administration is a major problem, however, the methodological destruction of the real economic sectors of the country is another one.. The research attempts to specify the main determinants of cash outflow from the banking sector in Sudan (during the period 1972-2011). Hence, those revealing the major impacts of the cash outflow on the economic activity and rates of inflation. However, chaotic economic policies as: incalculable privatization of state institutions and corrupt practices, false Islamization of the banking

3

sector with improper institutional foundations and corrupt economic and administrative governmental institutions, are not excluded as major part of the problem. The research hypotheses were:

(1) the Banks economic behavior of attainment reserves and expanding loans is main cause of cash outflow,

(2) the government financial activity to cover its budget deficits, and the effective demand for money liquidity by the public are the main factors transmitting the impacts of cash outflow to the major macroeconomic variables (Money stock, aggregate demand and supply, cost of resource adjustment, and the rate of inflation),

(3) Monetization of bank loans via allowing the growth in the effective demand for liquidity by the public directly leads to aggravation of inflation given the downward trend of money velocity,

(4) Monetization of bank loans via financing the current deficits of the government, causes an inflationary pressures due to aggregate demand expansion, the real side of the economy will not be affected.

Using twelve equations-mathematical model systems with endogenous variables: the demand for effective money liquidity, the nominal and real growth of money stock, the demand for real balances, cost of resources adjustment, the aggregate demand, Gross Domestic Product GDP, the capital stock, the private investment, rate of inflation, bank loans, velocity of wide money, and the current budget deficit. Moreover, the general price level index, the real output trend and its actual deviations from that trend, quasi money, real depreciation of the local currency, the labor force size, the private savings and excess reserves held by banks as exogenous variables were used.

Based on annual data of Sudan economy for the study period, iterative Weighted Two-Stage Least Squares (IWTLS) were applied through running an econometric computer program of E-views. The Results revealed that monetization in Sudan is mainly determined by the availability of Bank loans which in turn are affected largely by banks' ability to form excess reserves, by dominated the government borrowing, and less by liquidity preference of the public. Moreover, Money stock has great endogeneity. The bank loans expansion in Sudan economy may induce liquidity preference or may cause inflation through inducement of monetary growth by the BOS. Inflation growth may exceed the monetary growth. So, real money growth falls and thus de-accelerates velocity and causes economic recession. On the other hand, the bank loans expansions encourage the government to incur large deficits thus pulling the aggregate demand and aggravate inflation with no effect on the real side of the economy. The research recommended controlling the process of monetization, through controlling banks' ability to expand loans, good perception to the growth in liquidity preference, and sizing of the government borrowing. To control liquidity preference the government borrowing must be rationed and the policy must be of minimum impact on inflation. To avoid high liquidity preference associated with less velocity, the policy must be designed to facilitate bank loans to the prior productive sectors and the government borrowing must be rationed and real sources for financing deficits must be developed.

3. Introduction

The major interrelated goal of monetary and fiscal policies is to eliminate the disequilibrium and pressures from the aggregate demand. Aggregate demand has its serious influences on the rates of inflation, exchange rate system and then on the general equilibrium (Laxton et al, 1994). Thus, money plays an important role in modern economies. Accordingly, economists focus on how to develop means and tools to control and direct that money towards achieving the economic objectives. The ability of controlling money supply is surrounded by some doubts[1], because part of money is supplied by the banks from demand deposits which form part of the cash component. For this reason, although issuing of the cash component is controlled by the government, its ultimate distribution between bank and nonblank sectors are

---

[1] Uncertainty about the way private sector agents form their inflation expectations and exchange rate uncertainty (Conway, Drew, Hunt, and Scott, 1998); see also Drew and Hunt, (1999) who examined aspects of model uncertainty about potential output.

uncontrollable. Moreover, banks can change other assets such like treasury bills, longer-dated government securities and commercial bills to increase their advances, then increase money supply. So the authorities cannot directly control banks' credit because of their inability to control banks assets.

Theoretically, as noted by Maurer (2005) the distribution of cash between bank and nonblank sectors, depends upon the desires of banks, governments and the public to obtain and keep cash money. So the monetary authorities would intend to use various instruments to attain the required cash of the economy. In that case the popular instrument for the authorities is the interest rate. Some Islamic countries have alternative mechanism to the interest rate because of religious believes concerning the dealings through that instrument. The other instruments of control are; legal reserves ratio, internal liquidity ratio, profits margins, sectional credit ceilings and certificate of Musharaka of Central bank (CMCs). Most countries tend to keep their major proportion of cash money circulating within the banking system. The banking sector has an important role with regard to financial intermediation, attracting deposits, inducing investment and hence inducing the development process. However, in most LDCs the banking sector has, for a number of reasons, failed to carry on this task .

From the above-mentioned we draw the following facts:

1- Banks' Economic behavior of attaining its reserves and expanding of its loans is the main cause of Cash outflow from Banking sector in Sudan during the study period.

2- Both the Government financial demand to cover the budget deficit and the liquidity preference by the public are main factors transmit the impacts of Cash outflow to the rest of macroeconomic variables.

3- Monetization of Bank loans via allowing growth in liquidity preference by the public leads directly to inflation associated with a downward trend of velocity.

4- Monetization of Bank loans via financing current Budget deficit of the Government may lead to inflationary pressures due to expansion in Aggregate demand with no response from the real side.

5- Effectiveness of the available monetary policy instruments requires the property of high controllability and desirable influences on monetary, financial, and real sectors.

Thus, the research attempts to specify the main determinants of cash outflow from the banking sector in Sudan. Moreover, we focus on how to sort out major impacts of the cash outflow on the economic activity and rates of inflation. Accordingly, the research hypotheses were formulated as following:

1. The Banks economic behavior of attainment of reserves and expanding loans is the main cause of cash outflow.

2. The government financial activity to cover its budget deficits, and the effective demand for liquidity by the public are the main factors that transmit the impacts

of cash outflow to major macroeconomic variables such as money stock, aggregate demand and supply, cost of resource adjustment and the rate of inflation.

3. Monetization of bank loans via allowing the growth in the effective demand for liquidity by the public directly leads to the aggravation of inflation given the downward trend in money velocity.

4. Monetization of bank loans via financing the current deficits of the government, causes an inflationary pressures due to aggregate demand expansion, the real side of the economy will not be affected.

The research focuses on Sudan as an example of LDCs; the banking sector has been suffering from the shortage of cash over the last three decades. Measured by the ratio of broad money (M_2) to GDP the degree of monetization in Sudan reached 22% during the 1970s and 30% during 1980s, and reaching its highest level during the 1990s. At the same time the economic activities exhibited a downward trend, especially in the industrial sector. As a ratio of broad money, quasi money, in domestic currency, which includes investment and demand deposits as well as the margins on grants and letters of credit, has deteriorated from 17% to 8% in 1987 and 1997 respectively. The shortage of cash within the banking system produce the following impact on Sudan economy:

1. Aggravation of cash liquidity out of the Bank of Sudan (BOS) control.

2. Loss of banking sector of its role of financial mediation and failing to meet the required finance of Private sector development, which is regarded as one of the main aims of liberalization policies.

3. Cash scarcity in the banking sector induced more pressures on the BOS. So it tended to make advances to the government from unreal source of finance, which directly increase the cash in the economy, thus causing more inflation.

Furthermore, in its efforts to combat inflation, the monetary authority used both traditional and modern policy instruments, such as the interest rate, the reserve ratio, and the maximum credit ceilings to control money supply in general and the cash component in particular. The problem was then how to induce investment at low cost of borrowing (i.e., at low interest rates) while credit ceilings are under operation.

In this regard, the available studies such as Ahmed, M. O. et al (1998) and Mohamed Khare (2000) conducted during the last three decades indicated a number of major factors which contributed in deepening the problem of cash outflow in Sudan. These could be classified into tow groups, as follows:

1. Price factors, which include exchange rate, rates of inflation, and the returns on banks deposits.
2. Non-price factors, which include government temporary borrowing from the banking sector to cover the current budget deficit, banking sector violations of required cash reserves and credit ceilings and the public attitude towards instability of prices and economic policies, in addition to the phenomenon of refer to drawer checks (RD).

Zakaria, (1999) applied the special criteria for determining the ideal stock of money in Sudan. He argued that *"for the period (1989/90 - 1993/94) the growth rate of the money stock except for the year 1991/92 where the nominal GDP has grown by 108% corresponding to 143% for the stock of money"*. He concluded that inflation in the Sudan during that period is not purely are monetary phenomenon.

The Analytical method depended on utilizing the Weighted Two-Stage Least Squares (WTSLS), which its estimator is the two-stage version of the weighted least squares estimator described above. WTSLS is an appropriate technique when some of the right-hand side variables are correlated with the error term. Heteroskedasticity, is expected but no contemporaneous correlation in the residuals (Pindyck, R. S. and D. L. Rubinfeld (1998). An equations-mathematical model was proposed to identify major determinants of the following endogenous macroeconomic variables: demand for effective money liquidity, nominal and real growth of money supply, demand for real balances, cost of resources adjustment, aggregate demand, Gross Domestic Product GDP, capital stock, private investment, rate of inflation, bank loans, velocity of broad money, and the current budget deficit. The exogenous variables were: general price level index, real output trend and its actual deviations from that trend, quasi money, real exchange rate of local currency, labor force, private savings and excess reserves held by banks. The model estimation relied on the data of Sudan Economy collected on annual basis. An econometric method W2SLS applied to the specified model. That through using E-views computer econometric program. The main steps:

1- TSLS is applied to the un-weighted system to enforcing any cross-equation parameter restrictions.
2- Then, the results from this estimation used to form equation weights, based upon the estimated equation variances.
3- If there are no cross-equation restrictions, these first-stage results will be identical to un-weighted single-equation TSLS.
4- (Davidson, R. and J. G. MacKinnon, 1993 pp. 221–224) and (Johnston, J. and J. E. DiNardo, 1997).

We shall focus on the following objectives:

1- Identification of the main determinants of Cash outflow from the Banking sector in Sudan during the study period.
2- Sorting out the impact of Cash outflow from Banks on major macroeconomic variables.

4. Money Concept and Definitions

Authors of the Currency School[2] such as Loyd (1841) and Fisher (1913) considered that Money supply was generally viewed as the total of currency units in the economy. But such definitions do tell us about how to measure it. On the other hand positivists (monetarists and Keynesians) such as Friedman and Schwartz (1970) suggest that evaluation of money supply is mainly a

---

[2] "Currency School" is an English school in the 19th century. For this school of thought, boom is due to the issue of bank notes without metallic backing. Their main error is that they did not understand the current accounts played the same role.

question of econometric experimentation[3].

A proper definition of money supply is vital for both theories and applied economics, notably for the study of inflation, economic cycle, monetary and banking crises (Yuong Ha, 2000). As indicated by Shostak (1999)

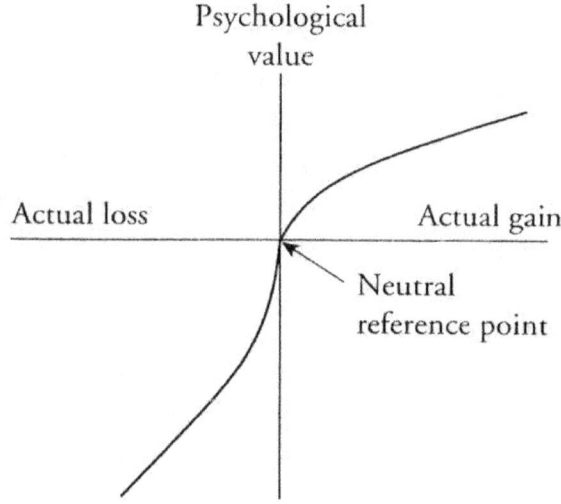

Fig.1 The value function of prospect theory. Reference: Soman, 2004

money could be of considerable use to businessmen who are involved in international financial operations and are interested in judging the risk of a crisis in a stock. Money is defined from two point of view, a priori definitions[4] which focus on the basic functions of money; as medium of exchange, unit of account, store of value, and means of deferred payments (Siegel, 1982). It has been defined by the Fed. Reserve Bank of Philadelphia (1997): *Money*

---

[3] The positivist approach is most useful in making predictions about observable phenomena on the basis of the theory accents. This approach is summed up in Friedman and Schwartz (1970).

[4] These is one of Austrian approach which based on subjectivism, a priorism, and verbal logic. It was criticized that they sometimes make money supply measurement difficult (See Nicolas Bouzou, N. D.).

bewitches people. They fret for it, and they sweat for it. They devise most ingenious ways to get it, and most ingenious ways to get rid of it. Money is the only commodity that is good for nothing but to be gotten rid of. It will not feed you, cloth you, shelter you, or amuse you, unless you spend it or invest it. It imports value only in parting. People will do almost any thing for money, and money will do almost any thing for people. Money is a captivating, circulating, masquerading puzzle. Thus, it could simply be defined as any thing that people generally will accept to satisfy debts (Dornbusch, 1990). On the other hand, Lloyd (1997) defined money that it is the stock of items used to make payments for goods and services. Lloyd (1997) argued more about money that it is most commonly defined and generally acceptable as payment for goods or services or for the discharge of debt. This definition is a behavioral one. It emphasizes the element of confidence (psychological factor involved in the concept of money). Moreover, the value function of prosperity materially depends on money. To use an item as money relies on our belief that it will retain its value or purchasing power and will continue to be acceptable. This confidence in turn relies on the assurance of reasonably strict limits on the supply of the item to be used as money.

Another point of view is known as *Pragmatic Definitions of Money.* This view focuses on the things that are used as money and its main characteristics. Trying to capture the problem of changing things that are employed as money through different times and different places, this is known as the positivists approach[5]. This trend was indicated by Friedman and Shwartz (1970, p.137) that the definition of money is to be sought for, not on grounds of principle but on ground of usefulness in organizing our knowledge of economic relationships. Therefore, "Money is that to which we choose to assign a number by specified operations; it is not something in existence to be discovered. It is a tentative scientific construct to be invented, like; length, or force in physics".

This concept of money raises the strong possibility that the group of assets that constitute our measure of money today is likely to evolve over time. That definition also is emphasized by Lecarpentier-Moyal (1998)[6]. For the *Essential Empirical Definitions*, before 1980, it was made to include: M_1 which represents current deposits at commercial banks **plus** circulated currency and coins. M_2 which, represents M_1 plus saving deposits plus small time deposits. M_3 represents M_2 plus saving deposits at thrifts institutions. Siegel (1982, p.65) summarized some embarrassments of economists concerning suitable definition of money. He argued that the failure of a priori definition of money entry, by subdividing assets on bases of medium of exchange and store of value, refers to the

---

[5] in contrast, Positivists (monetarists and Keynesian) suggest that the evolution of money supply is mainly a question of econometrics experiments, their methodology is based on statistical correlations.

[6] He argued that the aim is to define weighted aggregates taking into account the degree of moneyness (i.e. the substitutability between financial assets and what is widely considered as money). Hence financial assets can be substituted for money as medium of exchange and reserve of value, but at different degrees. These degrees have to be quantified so that the aggregate can be weighted.

existing differences in assets bases. Whereas, pragmatic entry of definition of money attempts to link the most appropriate money aggregate with economic activity. This entry also, failed to attain solid and absolute definition.

In the context of setting a stable definition of money Seigal (1982) explained that modern definitions of money take into account the trend of legal changes, modern functions of banks, and non-bank institutions development. So, broad definitions of money include all deposits held by depository institutions. For that, modern M2 and M3 differ in components from older ones. Components as financial quotas of money market, Repurchasing Agreements (RPAs), and Eurodollar deposits have been included.

The Recent Empirical Definitions in modern economies as USA, have vast variety of financial assets, from currency to complicated claims on corporations. There are four main monetary aggregates as indicated by Dornbusch and Fischer (1990): currency, M_1, M_2, and M_3. These components of monetary aggregates could be described as follows :

1. Currency: Consists of coins and notes in circulation.
2. Demand deposits: Non-interest-bearing checking accounts at commercial banks, excluding deposits of other banks, the government, and foreign governments.

3. Traveler's checks: The total comprises only those checks issued by non-banks. Traveler's checks issued by banks are included in demand deposits.
4. Other checkable deposits: Interest- earning checking accounts, including NOW and ATS accounts. ATS stands for automatic transfer from saving accounts.
5. With ATS a deposit holder keeps assets in a saving account, and the bank transfers them automatically to the checking account $M_1 = (1)+(2)+(3)+(4)$,
6. Overnight repurchase agreements (RPAs): Borrowing by a bank from a nonblank   customer. The bank sells a security e.g., a treasury bill to today and promises to buy it back at fixed price tomorrow.
7. Overnight Eurodollars: Deposits that pay interest and mature the next day.
8. Money Market Mutual Funds shares: Interest-earning checkable deposits in mutual funds that invest in short-term assets. Some MMMF shares are held by institutions; these are excluded from M_2 but included in M3.
9. Money market deposit accounts: MMMFS runs by banks, with the advantage that they are insured up to $100, 000. They were introduced at the end of 1982 to allow the banks to compete with MMMFs.
10. Savings deposits are at banks and other thrift institutions that are not transferable by checks. They are often recorded in a separate passbook kept by the depositor.
11. Small time deposits: Interest-bearing deposits with a specific maturity date. Before that date they can be used only if a penalty is paid (it is less than U$ 100,000): $M_2 = M_1 + (5)+(6)+(7)+(8)+(9)+(10)$

12. large-denomination time deposits: Interest-bearing deposits of more than US$100,000 denomination. The total excludes amounts held by MMMFs or other similar institutions so not to be twicely counted in the monetary aggregates.

13. Term repurchase agreements (RPAs): These are RPAs sold by thrift institutions, typically for longer than overnight. $M_3 = M_2 + (11) + (12) + MMMFs$ held by institutions

According to the American Official Monetary Aggregates Nicolas Bouzou (2000, p.16-18) described the following aggregation[7] for the money supply M1 consists of:

1. Currency outside US Treasury, the Feds, and vaults of depository institutions.
2. Travelers' checks of non-bank issuers.
3. Demand deposits at commercial banks(other than those due to depository institutions, US Government, foreign banks, and official institutions. Less cash items in process of collection and federal float).
4. Other Checkable Deposits (OCDs), include; Negotiable Order of Withdrawal (NOW) accounts and Automatic Transfer Services (ATS) accounts at depository institutions, credit union share draft accounts and demand deposits at thrift institutions.

M_2 consist of M1 plus:

1. Deposits in money market deposit accounts.
2. Time deposits (small denomination) including Retail Papers (RPs) accounts.

---

[7] Publications of the Statistical Reserve of the Board of Governors of the Federal Reserve System (the Fed.), March 16, 2000.

3. Balances in Money Market Mutual Fund shares (MMMFs). Less Individual Retirement Accounts(IRA)and Keogh balances at depository institutions and MMMFs.
4. M3 consist of M2 plus:
5. Large denomination Time deposits (not less than US $100 000).
6. Balance in institutional money funds.
7. Retail Papers (RPs) liabilities (overnight or term held by US residents or foreign branches of US). Less accounts held by depository institutions, the Government, MMMFs, foreign banks and institutional money funds balances.

The classical aggregate model neutralizes the role of money in the economy. But the successive models demonstrate that money plays an important role in the determination of income and employment. Is-Lm model try to pay attention to the interaction of goods and assets markets. In the past, the focus was on income determination, through the argument that income affects spending, which in turn determines output and income. Then IS-LM model discusses the effects on spending, and thus income through the mechanism of interest rates, and the dependence of assets markets on income. Conceptually, the higher income raises money demand and thus interest rates. Moreover, the higher interest rates lower spending and thus income. Finally, spending, interest rates, and income are determined, jointly, by an equilibrium in goods and assets markets (Dornbusch, 1990, p.108).

With regard to the importance and unimportance of money, Lloyd (1997, p.17) argued about concerning the unimportance of money, that what determines a nation's standards of living is the capacity of its people to produce goods and services. If we suddenly double the amounts of goods and services that we collectively produce, our real income and standard of living will collectively double. If instead we double the amount of money (currency, coins, and checking accounts) existing in the nation, we would not be better off. That is because, our ability to produce goods and services would not be enhanced and the living standards would not improve. At the same time, inflation unleashed by excessive expansion of money supply, damage the nation's well being.

Concerning the importance of money, Lloyd (1997, p.17) argued that money could be viewed from an opposite angle, because money facilitates the process of exchange, allowing for more efficient operation of the economy, and raising the standards of living. If there is an excess quantity of output in the economy, money facilitates its exchange to avoid the extremes of depression. Moreover, money minimizes inflation and maintains the environment in which economic activity can flourish. Meanwhile, irresponsibly managed money can cause damage to the society. Money could be a positive force which contributes to the stability of economic variables; prices, income, and employment.

5. Money Functions and Forms

Concerning the function of money McConnell and Stanly (1993) defined money in the following expression: *Money is what money does, any thing that performs the functions of money is money.* ***Traditionally***, money has three major functions which could be viewed as unit of account, medium of exchange and store of value. With regard to its function as ***unit of account***, Silk (1975, p.352) mentioned, that money can be used as unit of accounts, enabling us to add together the disparate elements of goods and services that comprise Gross National Product (GNP). However, these could not be added directly, but when converted via money to money prices, their values could be easily added to each other. Thus money serves as a means of measuring economic activities. This measuring function facilitates exchanges of goods between buyers and sellers by permitting exact ratios to be worked out among all goods and services. In its role as a unit of account, money permits businesses to establish accounting systems that enable them to determine, precisely, their costs of doing businesses and the prices they should charge to realize profits. In that respect some economist such as Mises and Cantillon suggested that the quantity of money is relevant in helping the promotion of efficient allocation. That is true for the use of real resources at both micro and macro levels of the economy (Bouzou, pp.3-5). The second major function of money is its role as a ***medium of exchange***. Silk (1975, p.352) describes this function as: *If an economy is to benefit from increased production that comes from specialization and division of labor, it must have a well-developed exchange mechanism.* He emphasized that the simplest form of exchange is barter (direct trading of goods between people). If we rely on barter only there would be very little specialization in our world. Because, barter requires a double coincidence of wants and also fails with the problem of indivisibility of some goods to satisfy suitably the needs. In that case, if money introduced will solve the two mentioned problems, acceptance of money as a medium of exchange permits specialization and division of labor throughout a highly complex economy.

The third major function of money is its role as a *Store of Value*, which is closely related to its function as a medium of exchange. Because, it allows for exchanging the undesired properties with something that might be required later in future (money lets you wait and provide you for your future needs). Unfortunately, money is not a perfect store of value. Silk (1975, p.353) explains that: if prices rise, money will loose some of its value, and if prices fall, money will gain extra value. Shedding more light on this point, Silk notes that in times when people distrust money as a store of value, they will try to convert it into things that they think will be better stores of value such as; land, precious metals, ..., stocks,...etc. Conversely, when prices are falling, the value of money as a store of value shall be rising. People may convert the value of goods or assets whose values are dropping into money by selling it.

With regard to the *Forms of Money* an astonishing variety of things have been used as money through out history. Money has been created from any thing that is generally wanted and was in a convenient form that could be used as a medium of exchange. Beads, pieces of leather, wampum, elephant-tail bristles, various metals, and even wives have served as money in different situations. Money gains its value from the things for which you can exchange them. Lloyd (1997, p.18) tried to explain the forms of money arguing that traditionally, most economists defined money as all currency and coins held by the public, demand deposits, and other checkable deposits in commercial banks and saving institutions. However, in practice, money forms include all payments that are made by exchange coins and paper currency or by transfers of deposits balances via checks or electronic transfer. This last definition fits the conceptual notion of money as those items which are *"generally acceptable in making payments"*.

6. Money as a Component of Assets

As it was shown by Dornbusch and Fischer (1990, P.122) that assets fall into two broad categories; financial assets and tangible assets. A further subdivision identifies *four main assets categories* in the economy: money and other deposits (credit instruments), short run bonds, equities (stocks), and tangible (real) assets. The first categories of assets is *money and other deposits*. Money stock proper consists of assets that can be immediately used for making payments.

The second category of assets noted by Dornbusch and Fischer (1990) is *bonds* which is defined as a promise by a borrower to pay the lender a certain amount (the principal) at a specific date (maturity date) and to pay a given amount of interest per year in the mean time. Hence, the third category of assets is **equities of stocks**, and those are claims to a share of the profits of an enterprise. The share holder or stock holder, receives a certain amount as return on equities in two forms. Either in the form of regular dividends which means to receive certain amount for each share you own or in the form of retained profits (to be reinvested). The latter, makes the share more valuable. Because, new claims of profits added to the stocks' value. Therefore, the price of the stock in the market will rise thus, the stock holders can make capital gains (an increase per period of time in the price of an assets).

Finally, the fourth form is *the real assets*. Those are tangible assets such as: machines, land, and structures owned by corporations and consumer durables (cars, washing machines, stereos, ...etc), residences, ...etc. Those assets as indicated by Dornbusch (1990, p.124) carry a return that differs from one asset to another in the form of rents or profits. For that it can be divided into two main groups: financial assets which include money, bonds, and stocks, and real assets. Finally, he rearranges these categories by classifying assets into two groups. He puts in one side money with its specific characteristic as an only asset that can serve as means of payment. Meanwhile, all other assets on the other side. Money offers convenience of being means of payment. It carries a lower return than other assets. However, that differential depends on the relative supplies of assets, for when the Central Bank reduces money supply and increases the supply of other assets, the yield on the other assets increases.

7. Money and Economic Activity

In order to study the way that money affect the flow of economic activity as shown by Silk (1975, p. 367) and as recently also suggested by Maurer (2005, p.5) that money supply is currency and checking accounts. Some economists suggest Gross Domestic Product as measure proxy for macroeconomic activity. Dornbusch and Fischer (1990, p.35) illustrate economic activity as a flow of goods and services that occurs largely through affecting total spending.

Explaining the effect and transmission mechanism of money, Silk (1975) added that an increase in money supply affects total spending of the economy in part directly by putting more funds in the hands of consumers, businesses, and government units. Partially, the increases in money supply influence total spending indirectly by reducing rates of interest, there by making it cheaper and more attractive for consumers, businesses, and government units. Thus, to borrow funds, they will increase their spending on goods and services. On the other hand, reductions in money supply will cause reductions in total spending both directly, and indirectly by increasing rates of interest, which in turn make money more costly and discourage those economic agents from borrowing and spending.

The **Monetary theory** depicts an analysis of the relationship between the nation's money supply and economic activity. The main goal of monetary theory as pointed out by Ngatani (1982) is to provide satisfactory answers to the following questions: (1) What is the role of money in aggregate economy? (2) How does a change in money supply influence other important variables in the system? (3) How can such knowledge be utilized to prescribe policies?

8. Fundamentals of the Quantity Theory

Monetary theorists have long been interested in establishing the relationship between the money and the general level of price. The fundamental proposition of the quantity theory of money as indicated by such monetarists like Keynes and Freidman. That if individuals are free to desire their money holdings, which equal to that quantity provided by the authority. Therefore, prices and money income have to change to the extant that money holdings equal to its desired volume. In that case, a monetary equilibrium will be attained. The monetary equilibrium is a position where the demand for money adapts in response to that changes of prices and income. Therefore, the equilibrium condition realized when the demand for money equals quantity of money provided by both the monetary authorities and the banking system (Siegel, 1982, p.358).

The fundamental proposition of the quantity theory of money is that price level determined through nominal money balances supply and the demand for real money balances. The supply of nominal money balances depends on the implemented policies of monetary authorities and the banking system. Meanwhile, the demand for real money balances is determined by the public behavior. If the demand for money as medium of exchange determined according to specific plans to purchase certain package of commodities, then, the demand for real money balances will be also determined:

$$M^s = M^d = P \cdot m^d$$

Then monetary equilibrium require:

$$M^s = P \cdot m^d$$

That:

$$P = \frac{M^s}{m^d}$$

Last equation represents the quantity theory of money. Where equilibrium price level is determined the proportion of nominal money supply that predetermined by the authority and banking system. And the demand for real balances that determined by free choice of nonblank private sector.

The Cambridge equation has been developed by Cambridge economists such as Pigou, Marshall, Robertson, and Keynes. Cambridge group thought that superior liquidity of money offers utility to its holder as result of its convenience and security. However, the transaction demand for money is essential and important for Cambridge school of thought. It is necessary to link demand for money and the near future plan of spending on goods and services. Accordingly, as expenses financed by income, Cambridge equation would take the following formula:

$$m^d = Ky$$

Where:

m^d The demand for real money balances

y Real income that is proportion of nominal income to the prices index

K A proportion of income held by the public as liquid money. K may affected by the money balances held by the public, income receiving duration, transactions levels and vertical integration between industries.

9. The Money Income Theory

The equation of exchange is one of useful ways has been used to illustrate the connection between *money*

and *economic activity*, well-known *equation of exchange* take the following formula:

$$MV_T = PT$$

Where:

M   is the average money supply in existence in a given year.

V_T is money transaction velocity - that is, the number of that average dollar is spent per year i.e.($V_T = PT / M$).

P   is the average price of the transactions that take place during the year.

T   is the number of transactions occurring during the year.

Fisher (1913, p.17) developed the equation of exchange. Clarifying the role of money in the economy. In his book *The Purchasing Power of Money*, he detailed the factors that influence the *money transaction velocity* and real output. Because Fisher believed that velocity and real output change slowly. He argued that the principle cause of inflation and deflation is changes in the quantity of money. To conduct monetary policy Lloyd (1997, p. 495) wrote that Fisher contributed to the development of economics as a science. By paying more interest to the final goods and services, instead of the volume of transactions in every thing; bonds, stocks, raw material, used car, and other sale items. To avoid doubling of accounts, Fisher remarked that it is useful to reformulate the equation of exchange in terms of expenditures on final goods and services only. The formula is:

$$MV_Y = PY$$

Where:

M   is the average money stock exist in a given year.

V_Y is money income velocity, or the number of times the average dollar is spent on final goods and services per year ($V_Y = PY/M$ **or** $= GDP/M$).

P   is average price of all goods and services purchased during the year i.e. average price of all goods and services constituting GDP, or an index of such prices relative to some base year.

Y   is a number of final goods and services purchased in the year, or an index of real GDP relative to the base year.

In this formula the nominal GDP expenditures in a given year is average money supply multiplied by the annual rate of turnover of money, and also, stands for aggregate spending on final goods and services. The equation in itself tells nothing about the real world behavior. It makes no assertions about the causal relationships among its four variables. Nevertheless, this equation provides a useful framework for thinking about the role of money in macroeconomic analysis, it indicates that if money supply changes, one of two things must happen: (1) the velocity of money (V_Y) must change proportionally in the opposite direction, so that, GDP expenditure, nominal income or money values of expenditures remain unchanged. That is in accordance with Anderson and Hazlett view in (Blanchette, 2005), (2) the GDP expenditures must move in the same direction as money supply. Putting in mind that GDP expenditures may increase also as result of an increase in money velocity(V_Y). At one hypothetical extreme, if the velocity (V_Y) is constant, money supply is the sole determinant of the level of nominal GDP expenditures (economic activity). That postulation is in agreement with Anderson' theory[8] (Blanchitte, 2005). In that case, the only accurate tool to control GDP expenditures is money supply (Lloyd, 1997, p. 498). If the velocity (V_Y) is not constant there are two cases: (1) When the velocity fluctuates in reasonably good predictable manner, monetary policy can still be a highly effective method of influencing economic activity, (2) When the velocity fluctuates in a totally unpredictable way changes in money supply by the Central Bank will have no predictable effect on GDP expenditures, thus, monetary policy be would totally ineffective.

10.   Keynes' Theory of Money

Another route of connecting money with economic activity is *Keynes' theory of money*. Nagatani (1978, p.196) remarked on his book that Keynes was once a quantity theorist viewed like all others, that the determination of price level results from the two independent forces: (1) the behavior of the banking system determining the nominal balances. (2) the behavior of the public choosing an optimal stock of real balances. Then he determined the real balances as the

---

[8] Anderson's Theory of Money argues that this concept of "velocity of circulation" has very little importance to the science of economics, and certainly little impact on the level of prices. He writes:

"To me velocity of circulation seems to be a mere name, denoting, not any simple cause or small set of causes, which can exert a specific influence, but rather a meaningless abstract number, which is the non essential by-product of a highly heterogeneous lot of activities of men, some of which work one way, and others of which in another way, in affecting prices".

ratio of these two quantities, given by the following form:

$$M/P = m_1 + hm_2 \text{ or } P = m/(m_1 + m_2)$$

Where :

h   is a proportion of the banks' cash reserves to their deposits.

P   is a price of a consumption unit.

m_1 is a number of consumption units which the public required in cash.

m_2 is a number of consumption units which the public requires in bank deposits. Notice that m_1 and m_2 will depend on community's wealth and habits.

Accordingly, Keynes (1930) stated that the level of factor prices, directly, determines the price levels or the price level of output as a whole, independently of the banking system. Thus, if money matters, it should be by affecting profits through the bank rate[9], the phenomenon he called the *tertiary effect*. Some limitations could be taken for the above formula: (1) ignoring of expenditure for non consumption purposes, (2) failure to allow for variety of reasons for which banks deposits were held. In his process to investigate about the determinants of real balances, Keynes (1930) gradually moved away from conventional quantity theory. At first, Keynes defined the community's money income as the earnings of the factors of production or the cost of production (wages, salaries, the normal remuneration of entrepreneurs, interest on capital, and regular monopoly gains and rents). The difference between the actual and normal

---

[9] The bank rate is a term used by Keynes to denote for the interest rate through which money makes its effects on the banking system. Rise of this rate produce a fall in the private investment relative to the saving, the theory credited to Wicksell (cit. Nagatani,1978, p.200).

remuneration of entrepreneurs is called profits. Thus, profits is not a part of community's income. The normal remuneration of entrepreneurs defined as the rate of remuneration which, if entrepreneurs were open to make new bargains with all the factors of production at the current prevailing rates of earnings that would leave them under no motive either to increase or to decrease their scale of operation (Keynes, 1930). Keynes defined savings as a difference between the community's money income and its money expenditure on current consumption, while investment is the net increment of the capital of the community. The value of investment is therefore equal to the sum of savings and profits.

After presenting his fundamental equations, Keynes (1930) drew a conclusion that the price levels in equilibrium is largely independent of behavior of the banking system. Thus, money matters primarily by affecting the profits and makes its effect felt in the system chiefly through bank rates. Keynes (1930) thought that a rise in bank rate. would cause investment to decline relative to savings. Accordingly, the primary effects of a rise in bank rate is a fall in the price of fixed capital goods, and therefore, in the price of new investment goods and an increase in savings. Keynes explained more that a secondary effect will be a fall in the output of new investment goods and a fall in the price of consumption goods, due to the fall in the expenditure for consumption. Indeed the price of consumption goods will fall further due to the fall in incomes of the producers of investment goods (*tertiary effect*). In this stage, there would be a fall in price of both consumption and investment goods. Consequently there would be losses to all classes of entrepreneurs and decline the volume of employment offered to the factors of production at existing earnings. If the earnings (factors price) adjust downward smoothly at that occasion, a new equilibrium will be established at lower prices and lower rates of remuneration. If not, a state of unemployment will result and continues until the bank rate reversed its direction to be down or by chance something happens to alter the bank rate nature. On the other hand, Keynes (1930) viewed the problem from the point of view of the demand for money. He divided the total requirements of the monetary circulation between the industrial circulation and the financial one.

The first refers to that portion of requirements which relates to the business of maintaining the normal process of current output (distribution, exchange, and paying of the factors of production). The industrial circulation consists of: (1) the cash and deposits that workers carry to meet their personal expenditure (income deposits) and (2) the cash and that portion of business deposits which is directly related to the process of production and distribution. This circulation is expected to bear stable relation to the community's money income.

The second (financial circulation) relates to the business of holdings and exchanging of existing types of wealth including stock of exchange and money market transactions, speculations and the process of conveying current savings and profits into the hand of entrepreneurs. It consists of : (1) savings deposits (2) that portion of business deposits held for purposes of speculations in capital goods, commodities, and financial transactions. This circulation is largely independent of the money income but, depends on bank rate and the state of expectations which affect profits. Since the state of expectation affects the financial circulation, the connection between the bank rate and financial circulation seems to be indirect.

Keynes concluded that contrary to the Quantity theory of money, the total quantity of money would not be associated with any stable or invariant manner either with the level of bank rate or with the level of prices (Nagatani, 1978). That is mainly because, of Keynes' doubtfulness of the smooth adjustments in factor prices. So, the monetary authority should primarily be setting the level of bank rate rather than the total quantity of money. However, even with full capability to manipulate the level of bank rate the authority would have only a partial influence on the level of prices for it has no means of acting directly on the first term of the fundamental equations of Keynes. Moreover, in order to stimulate entrepreneurs via changing the availability of credit and abnormal profits and losses is likely to be very costly. With regard to the *Friedman's restatement of the quantity theory of money* (Friedman, 1956). He emphasized that the quantity theory of money was a theoretical approach that insisted money matters. He built his essay on two bases; the theoretical part and the empirical one.

Theoretically, after a general discussion of the nature and scope of assets choices by the ultimate wealth owing units, Friedman defined a general demand functions of money. To accept monetarist point of view, he admits that the money demand function is highly inelastic with respect to the variables which determine the velocity of money or fixed – namely the interest rates. So, Friedman's restatement was strongly criticized by various economists, from inside the Chicago School, Harry Johnson (1965, p.396) wrote that "...*to admit interest rates into demand function of money is to accept Keynesian revolution and Keynes attack on the quantity theory*". Moreover, Patinkin (1965) disagreed that "*Its title not withstanding, this is actually much closer to the Keynesian theory than the quantity theory ,the latter paid little attention to the possible impact on the rate of interest or shifts in tastes relating to the form in which assets are held*".

In any case, Friedman was not taking the issue with Keynesian at theoretical level only, he clarified that interest rates are real phenomena and that interest elasticity of demand for money is quite small (in the region of – 0.15). Hence, any change in the real sector can be absorbed into the velocity of money component with little harm.

 Moving to the empirical part, as Nagatani (1978, p. 204) briefly mentioned that there is a number of prepositions that quantity theorists accept:

1. The money demand is highly stable.
2. The demand function for money plays a vital role in determining such important variables as the level of money income or prices.

3. There are important factors affecting money supply that do not affect demand for money. This fact, along with the stability of demand for money function, enables one to trace out the effect of changes in money supply and collecting all these.

4. Income velocity of money possesses an extra ordinary empirical stability which makes it the centerpiece of macroeconomic analysis.

11. Monetary Policy and Economic Goals

Lloyd (1997, p.4) pointed out that the most important player in the money supply process that leads to short-run fluctuations is central bank. Indeed it is also clearly responsible for the long-run or trend behavior of money supply. Moreover, the central bank conducts monetary policy by implementing certain instruments that deliberately change the availability of credit, the level of interest rates and the money supply. It is most noticeable that monetary policy itself may result in fluctuations in prices and quantities. In general, as noted by Chung (2000, p.17) that to prevent the occurrence financial crises, the central bank should try to reduce macroeconomic fluctuations by consistency in its conduct of monetary policy. Most economists[10] would

---

[10] See also Lloyd (1997, p.440) who mentioned the ultimate objectives of the Fed are four: achievement of a relatively stable prices, maintenance of a high employment level, fostering of a stable Dollar Exchange Rate vis-à-vis the currencies of other nations, and encouragement of long-term economic growth. Noting that other goals such as maintenance of a

agree with the following list of economic goals, as indicated by Anthony (1974, p.294) that they would not necessarily agree on their order:

(1) full employment.

(2) reasonable price stability.

(3) an acceptable rate of economic growth.

(4) an equitable distribution of income.

(5) a high degree of economic freedom.

(6) the provision of economic security. and,

(7) stability in trade relations and a balance of payments equilibrium.

This list of goals is challenging enough to be fulfilled because of the following reasons. The first, is that some of these goals are in conflict, for example the specification of acceptable rates of economic growth as a goal may contradict the goal of equitable distribution of income. Moreover, the latter may conflict the goal of economic freedom. In addition to that probability of conflict between goals. The contradiction may occur between these goals and other parts such as; environment, population, religions, and the society. There also may be controversy over the goals that are to

---

stable interest rates and financial markets, are of importance as far as they contribute to the ultimate goals.

be satisfied[11] and how to set a national priorities. Finally, the problem of setting priorities themselves involves different government elements; branches, system of governance, changing political conditions, shifts of power, and role of personalities in swaying public opinions, all these form what is known as institutional lags. However, the link between policy tools and its goals or objectives is highly uncertain and variable. Its effects may take a year or long to impact aggregate output, employment, and price level. For this reason the CB aims instead for certain intermediate targets that are thought to be strongly linked to exogenous expenditures and the CB ultimate policy goals (appendix 3, figure 1). Then, the axial question is what is the ultimate goals of the CB?

Lloyd (1997, p.440) summarized the following ultimate goals of the CB policy ; achievement of a relatively stable price level, maintenance of a high employment level, fostering of a stable domestic currency rate, and encouragement of long term economic growth. The first major policy goal is to achieve, relatively, *stable Price level*, because, inflation has negative consequences on the economy. One of its impacts is redistribution of income in favor of some people, impairing others' purchasing power. As a result, tensions among various group of the society are created. Moreover, inflation creates uncertainty which, in turn, reduces investment

---

[11] Oddly enough, the controversy over the independence of central banks has provided the context for the discussion on which structure of incentives would best motivate central-bank officials to develop the correct monetary policy. For more details on that see De Soto (2006, p.660).

and slows long term growth of aggregate capital stock. Then, it slows the improvement of living standard and miss allocates resources which creates discrepancies of behavior. Finally, efficiency of price mechanism will be reduced.

The second goal of monetary policy is to *maintain a high level of employment.* Conceivably, because unemployment deprives families' income and increases social problems such as crimes and mental illness. Moreover, much people will be at the lower end of the income scale: reductions in output, income and taxes revenues. This goal could be achieved through influencing aggregate spending and level of total output.

The third goal of monetary policy is to *foster a stable domestic currency exchange rate.* Because, devaluation of currency exchange rate may impair the domestic economic activity, raising inflation, ... etc. Meanwhile, overvaluation of a currency affects export volume make it less competitive. Concerning exchange rate arrangement[12], Barrel et al (2003) viewed that to

---

[12] A fundamental issue that any exchange rate arrangement needs to handle. It is generally assumed to that real exchange rate will appreciate in all the candidate countries during accession period, due to both rapid productivity growth and nominal price convergence. During a period of convergence of productivity on European Union levels faster productivity growth in more open sectors pushes wages up across the economy as a whole. This puts upward pressure on prices in the no tradable sectors and hence observed inflation is higher the more rapid is productivity convergence. That is what called the Balassa-Samuelson effect of productivity on the real exchange rate (see Égert, 2001). The real appreciation associated with productivity can be seen as an

appreciate the real value of a currency, rapid productivity growth and nominal price convergence must be attained. Barrel et al (2003, pp.36-38) drew a conclusion that flexible exchange rate regime offers greater stability in the face of the shocks. The larger the cycles are, the less flexible the economies, the less openness , and the less financial advanced they are. Hence, they described the appropriate regime as a regime which depends on the anticipated shocks, has an ability to absorb shocks and puts in its consideration all the shocks that might arise. These results are in accordance with that in Barrel and Durry (2000). Moreover, the choice of the regime depends on the nature of shocks anticipated and the structure of the economies.

The fourth goal of monetary policy is to *encourage long-term economic growth*. Long-term economic growth is crucial because it determines the fate of living standards over a long time. Jones (2004, pp.1- 4) argued that enormous increase in standard of living over a century or two ago increased by a factor of about 10 or 20. Now new Standards of life quality such as refrigeration, electric lights, telephones, ..., skyscrapers and air conditioning. Concerning the central bank role in economic growth, Levine (1997) reported that it must foster a stable financial climate at low inflation level. Doing such to facilitate low level of long-run interest rates and high

---

equilibrium path, though the case for a real appreciation can also be supported on the basis of disparities in Purchasing Power Parity that have to be removed to produce an equilibrium.

level of investment. The CB must determine the physical stock and human capital, skills and education embodied in the workforce, investment in plant, equipment and rate of technological change. These are key variables to log-term economic growth. Moreover, the CB has to maintain economic stability and preventing severe economic downturns (Lloyd, 1997).

12. Monetary Policy Tools and Targets

The meaning of monetary policy as it was shown by Dornbuusch and Fischer (1997) is that *"we are concerned with the effect of an increase in the real quantity of money on the interest rate and level of income; through monetary policy the Central Bank (CB) affects the quantity of money and thereby the interest and the income"*.

The most important functions of the Central Bank (CB) are the regulation of the money supply and the control of the cost and availability of the credit through the use of deliberate and discretionary actions (Anthony, 1974). So, the CB has three main instruments to get control over money and credit; open market operations, reserve requirements, and the discount rate policy. Those also are Known as general monetary policy instruments. Open market operations is used to affect the volume of credit in the economy. According to Dornbusch and Fischer (1997) in the ***open market operations*** (OMO) the CB purchases bonds in exchange for money, thus, increasing the stock of money, or it sells bonds in exchange of money paid by the purchasers of the bonds and reducing money stock. Moreover, Reserve requirements is an instrument through which the CB can affect the structure and volume of deposits, money supply and lending. The Changes in the *Reserve Requirements* is a way to gain control over the money supply, by requiring banks to maintain a stated percentage of their deposits as reserves; it limits their ability to lend out funds and thus, their ability to create money by some multiple of deposits. It follows that the prime target of the CB policy will be the level of banks reserves, via required reserve ratio lowering of this ratio more funds are made available for lend, while raising of it less funds are available. However, this policy instrument is powerful, in case of lowering availability of funds.

The CB also has an instrument that can affect directly the volume of monetary base Known as discount rate. Also, through this instrument the CB exerts some indirect control over bank reserves willingness or unwillingness to lend through the *Changes in the Discount Rate*. Banks may find themselves in difficulties from time to time, either because they violate or choose to violate the reserves requirements or are faced with unforeseen local conditions that threaten to disturb their operations. So, they may either liquidate some assets to meet the situations or borrow from the CB by discounting some of their customers' obligations or by securing advances via an appropriate collateral. The policy of the CB in this case is called the discount rate. So, by fluctuating this rate the CB can encourage or discourage such advances and thus, affect the level of reserves.

These are general instruments that the CB work to influence money markets. The CB can openly announce its intentions to be receptive or directly squeezes loans and advances. The three instruments of monetary policy could be used singly or in combination. They need not all be used in every case, but, their coordination is required to achieve the maximum results. Besides, the CB also has *selective credit controls* that affect the way that credit allocated among diverse economic activities (Siegel, 1982). Among that is *Margin requirements*, the CB can set margins for purchasing stocks and bonds in their markets. These credit instructions must be followed by all dealers in that markets. Stock and bond purchasing margin defined as a difference between market value of a financial asset and its maximum loans available to finance its purchases. The CB intend to intervene in stock and bond markets so as to control the speculative activities, maintain a suitable credit position, limit the abnormal changes in financial asset prices and its un expected effect on the economy.

Another selective credit control to bring equilibrium among economic sectors is specific credit controls. Among those facilities, the CB may implement diversified credit costs, volume, and maturity periods. Moreover, may use higher interest for financing some sectors, diversify credit quotas, differentiated loan maturity and regulate large loans. Those facilities may not effect the credit availability but may encourage certain sort of credit that may have favorable effects on certain economic activities. The *Regulation Q* include the CB capability to enforce higher interest rates on consumption and time deposits at banks and other depository institutions. It was implemented in 1933 so as to support deposits guarantee plan. conversely, that was very cost for both banks and other depository institutions, though banks were relatively less effected. In general that regulation had led to less investment returns on deposits and less profits. In addition, the regulation brought, at that time, lack in competition and the funds were directed from those regulated depository institutions to those unregulated.

Finally, policy makers may attempt to pursue banks and other financial institutions to follow certain desirable directives in their economic activities that is what is known as *Moral persuasion*. In general open mouth policy may create no unless it is supported by other facilities. According to Lloyd (1997) to monitor the central bank's week-to-week progress in attaining policy goals, it needs to employ a variable that responds sensitively to the CB policy tools, which will influence, strongly, aggregate spending, thereby helping to achieve policy goals. Concerning the appropriate variables to be selected as *intermediate goals* of monetary policy, no consensus exists as to which variables the CB should attempt to control during a given period in order to achieve a goal (Batten et al, 1979). Suppose an economy is in a severe recession and the CB desires to implement a stimulating monetary policy. The CB could employ targets in term of its policy tools say, 10% growth rate of its portfolio of government securities or a 0.1% reduction each month in the percentage reserve requirements applicable to the demand deposits. Since the CB has total control over its own securities portfolio and reserves requirements, it will be feasible to achieve these desired magnitudes with precision. The problem with this approach is that the impact of a given change of that tool on aggregate spending and its ultimate policy goals is highly uncertain (Shuetrim and Thompson, 1999). Their rigid changes may be reinforced or counteracted by other factors e.g. the 10% growth of securities. It may be timed by zero or negative increases of banks reserves. However, many factors other than CB influence the monetary base M1, M2, reserves, and money supply (Schabert, 2005) [13].

---

[13] Schabert analyzed the relation between interest rate targets and money supply in a rational expectations equilibrium of a standard cash-in-advance mode, examining contingent monetary injections that people pay less attention to the behavior of monetary aggregates. The supply of reserves in open market operations, nevertheless, serves as the main instrument of most central banks. The supply and the demand for (narrow) money can thus be viewed to be "relevant only to the question of how the central bank must adjust the instruments under its direct control so as to implement its interest-rate operating targets"

According to Lloyd (1997, p444) a good *criteria for an effective Intermediate Targets* of the CB policy is that must be measurable, controllable, and important determinant of aggregate spending on final goods and services. *Measurability* is an accurate timely measurement that is essential for a suitable target variable. For the CB cannot shoot for a specific target, as an example M2, if there is no way to get accurate reading of it. Nor can it hit targeted interest rates if continuous data of it is not available. Meanwhile, *controllability* as measure indicates that a useful target of the CB policy must be under control. Through which, it can influence very strongly the capability in the short-run. In other words, the target should not be endogenous or strongly influenced by such forces as economic cycles, inflation expectations and interest rates. Since the target must be a variable that is not significantly influenced by the economic cycle and other economic forces. Hence,

---

(Woodford, 2003, p. 106). Accordingly, the behavior of monetary aggregates seems to be irrelevant for the analysis of optimal monetary policy regimes, which are specified in terms of interest rate targets, as for example in form of Taylor rules. His findings in that paper showed that the theoretical relation between money supply and interest rate targets is less intuitive than expected. this assumption, which facilitates the macroeconomic analysis of monetary policy, can be viewed as a reasonable simplification, provided that it matters only for the impact of changes in money supply on interest rates. Otherwise, money market frictions might be non-negligible even for macroeconomic effects of monetary policy.

exogenous variables, are more appropriate as intermediate target. The CB may face some difficulties in dictating the magnitude of such variables. In the real world these variables neither exogenous nor endogenous totally. Such disagreement stems from the ability of the CB to exert short run control over various variables.

The final measure of the intermediate target is to have a relative *importance*. Behaviorally, the target should contribute significantly to the policy goals obviously. Even if the CB has full control over the target variable but found no influence on the ultimate goals of the policy, this variable is irrelevant. The loss from this misspecification is great; exerting efforts, exhausting time in the wrong direction. Moreover, the relevant variable may be affected by the influence of irrelevant variable and change direction. Lloyd (1997, p.447) showed how the CB policy tools exert an effect on its goals. The variables connecting tools to goals is divided into two categories: (1) short range objectives or operating targets which respond very quickly to the change in CB policy tools while,(2) intermediate range objectives or targets do not change until after the short range variables have moved. Both groups are believed to have significant links in the transmission mechanism of monetary policy. On one hand, *Short-range Variables* are in a close proximity to the CB policy tools, and the CB is capable of exerting a quick strong influence over them within a short time. This could be divided into two sub-categories (Yuong, 2000, p.4). The first category of the short-range variables is the *Bank Reserves* and *Monetary Base Measures* which transmit the impact of monetary policy as following:

(1) measures of banks reserves and the monetary base, which form a critical group of variables within the transmission linkage. When the CB implements open market operation these variables are affected more rapidly. Guillermo and Végh (1990, p.5) noted that this category include; banks reserves, the monetary base, non borrowed reserves, non borrowed base, in addition to discounts and advances (borrowed reserves) and the net free reserves. These variables provide an important link in the CB influence over economic activity. Suppose the CB wishes to promote an economic stimulus by purchasing securities which generate monetary expansion in the monetary base and reserves which in turn affect banks lending, triggering the demand expansion process, with rising money supply, falling in short term yields and increasing of economic activities. Concerning the superiority of banks reserves and monetary base to each other, probably the first is superior to the second because, banks reserves provide a more reliable indication of banks ability to extend credit and create money recalling that $B = R + Cp$, and the currency Cp held by the public so as a component of monetary base (B) might be so large which could generate larger volume of bank credit and money than the latter. Inversely, monetary base (B) might be superior to banks reserves (R) because changes in demand for currency by the public affect reserves but not the base

(B) which the CB can accurately control (Brunner and Meltzer, 1990, p.376)[14].

(2) Non borrowed reserves (R-A) and Non borrowed base (B-A): Both targets contain an endogeneity element because of discount window borrowing and other factors. The volume of discounts and advances exhibits a marked procyclical pattern; rises during economic cycle expansions and declines during recessions (Guillermo and Végh 1990, p.5, seq.). Because of that Lloyd (1997, p.449) mentioned that the monetary base and bank reserves fluctuate endogenously unless the CB systematically neutralizes the effects of changes in discounts and advances via aggressive open market operations. To eliminate this endogenous characteristic, some economists suggested subtracting discounts and advances from the total monetary base (B) and the total bank reserves (R) to obtain what is known as non borrowed base (B-A) and non borrowed reserves (R-A). So, it become closest to being 100% exogenous, and the CB can exert very accurate control over both.

(3) Discounts and Advances (A): Because of the availability of information continuously about the borrowing of depository institutions from the CB, this variable scores very high on the measurability criterion (Kausar Hamdani et al 1991, p.52, seq.). It is however,

---

[14] Brunner and Meltzer separate money and the credit market; therefore, the interest rate has to decrease two times to restore an equilibrium: one time to balance demand and supply on the so called "money market" and one time to balance demand and supply on the "credit market". That view is also supported by Maurer (2005, p.27) by arguing that since money supply of the banking sector is identical to its credit supply, its clear that money enters the economy only one-time via the credit market and can consequently give only one rise to a one-time decrease of the interest rate. Therefore, Brunner and Meltzer's flawed monetarist double count of Monetary policy.

highly endogenous and ranks poorly on controllability. Nor it is, tightly linked to the ultimate objectives of the CB policy. In concluding this Lloyd (1997, p.449) remarked that the CB adopted the discounts and advances, though they are poor as short range operating targets, not for their merits but rather for political reasons because, putting of short term interest rates targets may be faced by political criticism. So, employing of discounts and advances targets is an effort to minimize the exposure to attacks by politicians or other critics.

(4) Net Free Reserves (NFR): This is defined as aggregate excess reserves held by depository institutions minus the volume of discounts and advances. It is thought to be a better target than excess reserves because, the latter variable includes a relatively large and volatile proportion of borrowed reserves, (A). Historically, targets analysis showed that NFR have strong endogenous quality. as a result, the link between NFR and aggregate expenditures is unstable today this reduce NFR effectiveness as monetary target (Lloyd, 1997, p.445).

The second category of short-range variables are *money market yields* (appendix 3, figure 1). Those are determined by the supply and demand where the CB influences securities prices in the market via the demand side. This occurs through purchasing of securities on open market operations. which pushes up securities prices and lowers its yields, as well as its effects on banks' excess reserves above desired levels and the monetary base. With regard to the *intermediate-range variables*, Kasman (1992, p.5, seq.) postulated that those variables have more predictable effect on aggregate expenditures than do the CB short-range operating variables, though these variables are more difficult for the CB to control. Also, Lloyd (1997, p.451) discussed the merits of the monetary aggregates and long-term interest rates as intermediate targets, in the following two steps:

(1) Monetary Aggregates: Money supply gained an increasing acceptance as an appropriate target for monetary policy during 1970s and early 1980s. However, their luster dimmed after that, as a result of putting of tolerance ranges in which the growth rates of various money supply measures were to be maintained for a certain time. Nevertheless, a significant problem is confronting money supply aggregates as intermediate targets, because of its poor data quality and time lag of its availability i.e., weekly data for M_2, M_3, ... etc, are available with a two week lag. And even its data are available it tend to be subject to substantial revisions. Accordingly, its intra-weekly monitoring and control would be difficult. Furthermore, even if good weekly data were available, short run volatility in the money supply multiplier would make accurate weekly control of money supply quite difficult. Thus, it seems the shortest time horizon for the CB to control the money supply is one month, using averages of the weekly data (Freidman and Schwartz, 1963).

(2) Long term Interest Rates: These were believed to have a greater impact on spending decisions than the short ones. Investment in plant and equipment, housing, and other structures depend on long term interest rates. Thus long term interest rates are; the corporate bonds yield, the mortgage rate, and municipal bond yield,

which are potential candidates for selection as monetary policy targets. If, as an example, the CB wishes to bring down the long term interest rates as part of anti recession program, it would prefer purchasing of securities, namely bonds. The banks reserves will be boosted via banks buying of securities and bonds. If other variables remain constant, the CB move will tend to increase bonds' prices and lower their yields. The long term interest rates depend heavily on such endogenous factors as expectations, private credit demands, government borrowing, and flow of private saving. For this reason the CB cannot exert accurate near term control over the long term interest rates[15]. This argument supported by Eggertsson (2003) also Eggertsson and Ostry (2005, p.12).

13.   The Transmission Mechanism

Suppose the *absence of effective action* by the CB. For some reasons, the economy begins to boom and inflationary pressures appear. If the CB response is slow or he refrain from interfering, the market place will make its adjustments to squeeze out all the credit available to exploit the booming conditions. That feasibly can be

---

[15] Boosting long-term interest rates occurs through what is known as the Fisher effect which sates that the harder the CB tries to bring down long-term interest rates in the short run via stimulative policies, the greater will be the inflationary pressures and the induced upward pull of market forces on interest rates. The conclusion is that the effective way for the CB to foster low long-term interest rates is to pursue a protracted policy of moderation in the growth of reserves, the monetary base and the monetary aggregates.

done by using idle funds which may increase the money velocity or using excess reserves by banks, raising interest rates and ... etc. Banks at their maximum ability to lend may turn to the CB for loans. In that case, it may generate an increase of money supply given the discount rate. Accordingly, without monetary constraint inflation will proceed further (Sevensson, 1997). However, when *the CB acts* as usual through for example open market operations. By selling securities so as to reduce banks reserves, banks customers may still demand funds. Faced with declining loanable funds and rising demand for them, banks will search for means to exploit this chance. In that respect some may refuse that situation by reducing the amount of their loans to others. Those who pay high rates of interest may attempt to gain more reserves by selling assets (say bonds). According to Yuong Ha (2000, p.6) the price of those assets might be depressed and raise interest rates. On other hand, banks may find that it is profitable to borrow heavily from the CB if the discount rate remained constant.

However, a coordinated central bank policy will have to increase the discount rate as the market interest rate rises. So, banks find the source of funds drying up and the boom dampened (Peak and Rosengren, 1995). Also, the CB could increase reserve requirements but, this step is usually kept for a last resort. In recession periods, a reverse case may be expected. In either case, the use of monetary policy instruments calls for coordination. The fact remain that power over the management of money and credit as 100% reserve requirement view[16] is concentrated in the hands of a few men who may facilitate coordinated actions (De Soto, 2006).

With regard to the *monetary policy transmission mechanism*, Dornbusch and Fischer (1997, p.140) pointed out two essential steps, a process by which changes in monetary policy affects aggregate spending:

1.   An increase in real balances generates a portfolio disequilibria, i.e. at the prevailing interest rate and level of income. People are holding more money than they want. This causes portfolio holders to attempt to reduce their money holdings by buying other assets, thereby changing assets prices and yields i.e. changes in money supply leads to changes in the interest rates.
2.   The changes in the interest rates affects the aggregate spending.
With regard to the detail of above the analysis is often differ, an analysis such as in Yuong Ha (2000, p.4) who include more than two assets and a number of interest rates. While other analyses include the influence of

---

[16] The principal defenders of a private banking system based on a 100-percent reserve requirement and managed by a central bank include the members of the Chicago School in the 1930s and currently, Maurice Allais, a recipient of the Nobel Prize in Economics. Thus it is conceivable that in a free-banking system, isolated attempts to expand bank credit would be curbed relatively quickly and spontaneously by customers' vigilance toward banks' operations and solvency. Hence, constant reassessment of the trust placed in banks, and, more than anything that is to say the effect of inter-bank clearing houses.

interest rates on other categories of aggregate demand in particular consumption and spending of local government. Such analysis like the one conducted by Piñón-Farah (1998, p.4) which is known as the concept of real balance effect , that changes in real balances increases wealth and therefore consumption demand. Nevertheless, such effect would not be applied in case of an open market operations purchase, in which one is changed for another (say bonds for money) without changing wealth. In addition, real balance effect is less important empirically because the relevant real balances are only a small part of the wealth. So, Dornbusch and Fischer (1997, p.141) concluded their indications that through the mentioned above two critical links between real balances and the ultimate effect on income, changes in real money supply affect the level of output in the economy. This outcome implies that if portfolio imbalances do not lead to significant changes in the interest rates, for whatever the reason or if spending does not respond to changes in the interest rates, the link between money supply and output does not exist. Such explanation is supported by Schabret[17](2005, p.5).

---

[17]His analysis (base on new Keynesian model) leads to results which seem to be inconsistent with the conventional view (a rise in the money supply would be accompanied by a decline in the interest rate, both instruments indicate a monetary expansion). It was found that the relation between money supply and interest rate targets was less intuitive. In particular an increase in money supply is in general associated with higher nominal interest rates as a result of lack of a liquidity effect an expansionary money supply is accompanied by a change in the interest rate which looks a contraction monetary stance.

With regard to the *theories of Transmission Mechanism*, Lloyd (1997, 582) mentioned there is broad agreement that monetary policy has strong effect on economic activity. How ever, the manner in which its influences is transmitted is not clear. The reason is variety in channels of monetary policy as well as they subject to cyclical changes in response to institutional, regulatory and technological changes.

(A) Early Keynesian Views

In Keynesian analysis investment is determined by interest rate and marginal efficiency of investment - that is, the rate of return expected from additional unit of investment. Keynes believed that interest elasticity of investment is relatively low. That is, he thought that marginal efficiency of investment function is relatively steeper. Accordingly, monetary policy changes exerts a moderate influence on aggregate demand. Where fiscal policy actions exert more powerful influence over economic activity (Lloyd (1997, 584).

Early Monetarist view based on a stable link between money and other assets. In this view individuals and firms maintain a broad portfolio of assets, base on returns expected at the margins on such assets, together with their liquidity, individuals and firms maintain a portfolio equilibrium. If the CB increases money supply, this will create a disequilibrium among holdings of money, stocks, and bonds. This prompts individuals and firms to use their excess money to purchase more assets. In doing so they bid up stock and bonds prices via rising its expected returns and decreased interest rate vis-à-vis money holdings does the economy reach a new equilibrium. However, stimulative monetary policy may be subject to the prevailed economic environment, for if agents are highly attuned to inflation, acceleration of monetary policy may trigger an increase in expected inflation, leading to higher nominal long-term interest rates through Fisher effect. In that case stock and bonds prices will fall unless the monetary changes stimulates their expected returns to offset the effect of higher interest rates.

14. Consumer's Expenditures

Monetary policy believed to influence total expenditures several channels, including the effect of interest rates on durable goods expenditures, the effect of a change in wealth on all categories of consumption and the effect of a change in liquidity on durable goods expenditures. Stimulating monetary policy summarized as follows:

1- an increase in money supply the *interest rates* will fall, consumer durable goods expenditures rises and causes economic expansion.

2- not only the current income affect consumption expenditures but also *the wealth* or expected future income. Given the current income constant, an increase in wealth implies a rise in expected income, then raises current consumption. The effect to wealth can be channeled through another route that is, an increase in money supply boosts stock and bonds prices, rising financial wealth then consumption and economic activity.

3- *Liquidity* is an important concept for asset holders, a portfolio of financial and real assets is differ in their liquidity. The case with which they may converted to cash on short notice without appreciable cost. In general financial assets are more liquid than real assets. An increase in money supply interest rates fall along with rises in bond prices, stock prices are likely to follow, and the liquidity portfolios increases. As the prospect of financial distress is reduced, consumer confidence increases. Expenditure on consumer durables increases and GDP rises.

In sum, monetary policy influences aggregate consumer expenditure as well as investment expenditure by altering interest rates, wealth, and liquidity. Putting in mind the share of consumption in the GDP, the effect of interest rate on GDP will be significant. Monetary policy affect investment through four channels, they include interest rates, the availability of bank credit, the rate of stock prices inducing firms to issue new shares of stocks, and the role of stock prices in affecting banks ability to lend money, detailed as follows:

1- the *interest rate* channel is captured by simple

Keynesian framework. That if the CB alters interest rates by increasing money supply, will make investment projects view as profitable, affect mortgage payments thus affordability of new homes or build up incentives. All rise the investment by firms and GDP increases.

2- With regard to *availability of credit* it is noticeable that bank loans are "special", because large firms with well-established credit ratings have wide range chive between alternative source of funds to finance their purchases. They issue commercial paper, bond, or shares of stock, or they may borrow from banks. However, small firms lack funds because they lack that access. When the CB eases monetary policy, say by increasing securities purchases on open market operations, additional reserves will be formed in banks, they relax their credit standards, extending loans to firms, investment increases and GDP rises.

3- *Tobin's q* is a theory of investment developed by Tobin. He define q as follows:

$$q = \frac{\text{Market value of firms}}{\text{Replacement cost of capital}}$$

This expression, the nominator is value of stock in the market, the denominator is cost of replacing machinery, tools, maintaining buildings .... etc. If stock market has placed a high valuation on firms, q is high, firms can issue new shares of stock at good prices relative to the cost of replacing or supplementing equipment and buildings, in this case investment will be high. Therefore, stimulative monetary policy boosts stock prices, Tobin's q is high, induces investment by firms and GDP rises.

4- *Adverse selection, Moral hazard, and bank lending* is a channel through which stimulative monetary policy can affect economic activity. Averse selection occurs when those most in need of loans due to difficulties are the ones who seek and grant loans. An increase in money supply boosts stock prices, increases firm's net worth, reducing adverse selection and moral hazard problems and make banks more willing to grant loans. This will raise investment and enhance economic activity.

15.   Net Exports

Until the 1980s decade economists thought that monetary policy exert almost its effect on aggregate demand through its influence on consumption and investment spending. As a result of international trade development the shares of both exports and imports in GDP rise. Thus implications of monetary policy for export and import behavior cannot be ignored. Remember that importing goods and services includes transferring of money and securities to the world, more over, exporting goods and services implies transferring money and securities to the country from the world. The trade balance will exhibit deficit or surplus according to whether import or export is larger. Besides, a huge pool of financial capital exists worldwide. These funds can be shifted instantaneously to financial sector that offers the most attractive rates of return. Thus, stimulating monetary policy can endue such capital flows via depreciation of local currency exchange rate which in turn, raise net exports then affect GDP (Lloyd, 1997).

In describing monetary instruments above, many complicated factors were omitted, for monetary policy is faced with some problems such as the problem of timing, uncertainty, changing velocity and the problem of financial intermediaries. Here is a content of summary of these problems.

However, *the problem of timing* denote that to conduct monetary policy, namely in a dynamic economy, time cannot be ignored. As Anthony wrote (1974, p. 298) there are many lags in the conduct of monetary policy. In addition to that, how long and how important are these lags, remains a subject of considerable uncertainty and controversy. Furthermore, Anthony (1974) sorted out two classifications of lags that effect of monetary policy:

1. the inside lags which refer to all steps and time it takes to go from the first recognition of problem existence to the point where the policy begins to affect the economy. These lags could be subdivided into many parts, the important ones are: Knowledge of the authority about the conditions, recognition of the problem, meetings and discussing the problem, setting some accord as to what policy is to be followed, the time elapses between the policy and its effects on money market.

2. the outside lags which are concerned with the response of the economy to the changed monetary conditions resulting from monetary policy. That monetary authority may react to a situation by altering money market conditions. However, there are other economic units such as consumers, firms, government, ... etc. that must also alter their plans in the face of changed conditions. So, if these economic units do not change their behavior, the economy will not be materially affected and monetary policy to that extent would be inefficient. Monetary policy lag length is crucial for the effectiveness of it. In addition, reactions to monetary policy may be short in time such as the response to initiated policy at the beginning of recession that help the economy to restore. Finally, if the lag is long enough i.e., more than one year during recession, monetary policy may result in worsening the economic conditions when recovery begins.

T*he problem of uncertainty*, as denoted by Anthony (1974) in conducting monetary policy uncertainty problem emerges and could be aggravated by the imprecise art of forecasting. It is conceivably difficult at any point in time to know just where the economy is operating in terms of economic cycle. The evidences gathered in this field are conflicted from part of the economy to another. Some economists such as Drew and Hunt (1999)[18] showed that if we cannot determine where we are at the present, how much difficult it is to predict where we will be in the future. That issue was discussed

---

[18] They examined uncertainty about potential output.

also by Izard et al (1998) and Shuetrim and Thompson (1999) [19]. Accordingly, some economists[20] like Clarida (1998), and Rude Busch and Svensson (1998) emphasized the CB to follow a set of rules regardless the state of the economy. They concentrated on money supply growth as the key variable. They also, advocated that the CB expands money supply at the same annual rate as long run growth of the economy. That could be done by letting the money stock grow at 5% per year which is better than attempting to regulate money stock according to economic conditions. Those emphasize Friedman's conclusion (1970) that " *it is better to have rules than to rely on flexible policy; a steady growth in the stock of money is a superior policy to discretionary policy tools*".

Some other economists like Yung chung (2002)[21] and Leigh (2005, p.3)[22] have been converted to such rule, but

---

[19] They show that uncertainty about the persistence in the economy can lead to optimal policy that is more aggressive than optimal under certainty.

[20] A substantial part of their literature concentrates on the use of simple policy rules on small stylized models many of which are backward looking closed economy models.

[21] It is argued that with regard to the central bank's role in a currency crisis, much depends on whether the central bank possesses those powers and functions necessary for attaining financial stability. In that respect, although the Bank of Korea greatly contributed to resolving the banking crisis through flexible monetary policy and its role as lender of last resort, it could not play a leading role because it was striped of its supervisory powers shortly after the outbreak of crisis.

[22] Regardig the inflation target, Leigh (2005) wrote that the statements made by Federal Reserve policy makers over the past quarter century suggested that the inflation has a target as well as its fluctuated level. Since the Federal Reserve does not have an explicit target and since

many more resisted its appealing simplicity. For this group monetary policy may not be perfect but, flexible policies are better than strict automatic rules. If the economy is to be guided by rules, of what use is economic analysis? It is better to seek a deeper understanding of the economy than to rely on the rule book. So, the questions of lags and errors in forecasting are serious ones, and the appeals for improvements in our knowledge are certainly justified.

Thus, for the concerning *the Problem of Changing Velocity* some monetarists like Cantillon, Marshall, Pigou and Fisher[23], focus on the money stock as the key monetary variable, presume that the velocity of money will not change or nearly constant to the money supply the extent that it could be ignored as far as monetary policy is concerned. This sight ignores the effects of financial community. For that reason some monetarists such as in Friedman and Schwartz (1963) indicated that *"other things being the same, it is highly plausible that the fraction of their assets individuals and business enterprises wish to hold in the form of money and also in the form of close substitutes for money, will be smaller when they look forward to a period of stable economic conditions than when they anticipate disturbed uncertain*

---

inflation has changed noticeably over the past 25 years, the assumption of constant target seems overly restrictive.

[23] Irving Fisher as an example developed the concept of equation of exchange illustrating the connection between money and economic activity. Assuming stability of the transactions velocity of money, he proposed a stable relationship between money supply and nominal GDP.

conditions". Anthony (1974, p.300) postulated that if the CB pursues a tight money policy and restricts the growth of money and credit, it is important to know the direction of change in the money velocity so as to help the policy restraint. But if some ways are found to manage the available money supply, then, spending can continue at the same level. The effectiveness of monetary policy is thereby reduced, whether that policy involves the use of traditional weapons or of a fixed growth in money supply. In contrast, Keynesians[24] asserted that money velocity is not stable and not predictable. Accordingly, their contention is that money supply plays only a secondary role in macroeconomics.

Recent available literature focuses on the complexity of this issue from operational perspective, because the simple policy formulations have not involved, explicitly, many other monetary variables such as; the price level, interest rates, expectations. The evidence shown in the study conducted in Mark De Broeck et al (1997, pp.30-32) indicate that the various factors that affect conduct of monetary policy in countries in transition can be seen as weakening the link, at least in the short run, between monetary aggregates, and aggregate demand and inflation. A use-full indicator measuring the strength of this link is the variability of the income velocity. Since more volatile velocity translates into a less well defined short-term link between money growth and nominal

---

[24] See McConnell and Brue (1993, p.309).

income. Short-run volatility of velocity is to be expected in the presence of adjustments in administered prices, shifts between domestic and foreign assets, and temporary capital inflows. Quarterly data on velocity in a number of transition countries indeed show substantial short-term fluctuations. In addition, the monetary authorities is to consider such effects from monetary variables of new and changed institutions. Therefore, wide range of informational variables, shifts in velocity have broader implications for the choice of operational guidelines for monetary policy[25].

Even though the definition of money is subject to different interpretations (M1, M2, M3, ... etc), then what is money supply? How its velocity can be measured ? and against which definition of national income ? does inflation result in higher interest rates or the latter have some connection with the first ? and what are the consequent changes in the velocity as the interest rates change ? All these questions add extended shadows over the effectiveness of monetary policy which remains uncertain and controversial. What causes the velocity to change, then become a source of problem for the CB and the conduct of monetary policy.

T*he financial intermediaries* are regarded among the sources of the CB problems. Such financial intermediaries include saving and loans institutions,

---

[25] See The International Monetary Fund Publication, OCTWE/2005/PDF, Ch. V, p. 108-114.

mutual saving banks, insurance companies, and pension funds. As noted by Sellon (1992) that they deal in near money and the highly liquid assets held by the public. Concerning importance of financial intermediaries[26], Levine (1997) viewed that it important for the growth. Since banking system is the primary transmitter of the monetary policy effect. Then, low intermediation reduces opportunities for growth, since a fully operative banking system improves risk sharing. Moreover, it promotes efficient resource allocation and stimulates investment. However, it could be said that other financial intermediaries cannot create money like commercial banks but, it can affect money supply indirectly through their actions over which, the CB has little or no control[27].

One way a financial community responds as an example to a tight monetary policy. If the central bank tight the

---

[26] Lloyd (1997. p. 88) wrote about the role of pension funds and mutual funds in the intermediation process, that they stimulated the range of investment outlets for individuals and firms, expanded the range of alternatives open to deficit spenders. They have enhanced the efficiency of financial intermediation. In contrast, the growth of pension and mutual funds created transitional costs in the form of financial instability, experienced in the late 1980s and early 1990s. Moreover, increased competition reduced the profitability of banks and thrifts, increasing their exposure to adverse shocks such as the collapse of oil prices in the mid-1980s. Although the failure of many banks and thrifts in the late 1980s and early 1990s, their earnings and balance sheets have gradually witnessed improvement since the end of recession of 1990 - 1991. Today these institutions are relatively healthy, and bank failures are running at 20-year lows.
[27] The International Monetary Fund, Internet Publication, OCTWE, 2005, Ch. V, P. 106).

excess reserves of banks (the ability to make loans), curtails the increase in money supply by selling securities and the market interest rates rise, the banks will be faced with excess demand for loans and will seek to satisfy them in order to gain high rates of return; selling government bonds, paying high interest charges. Then, the main question remains as how the velocity can be affected ? Banks usually have the ability to transfer quickly idle funds to be active and also pay high interest rates (Hörngren[28], 1985, p.203). While interest rates rise, financial intermediaries switch their holdings from government bonds to other assets because that yields a higher return. Moreover, they attempt to increase funds by raising their payment for deposits. Converting their idle funds to active one and investing it in mortgages and higher yielding assets. Accordingly, velocity of money will increase (Lloyd, 1997, p.527).

Households reduce their demand deposits and shift funds to interest earning deposits. In addition, they may begin to use credit cards more intensively. Corporate treasurers find ways to economize on cash holdings by

---

[28] Questioning about the efficacy of regulatory monetary policy Hörngren (1985) argued that regulatory measures are typically selective and limited to commercial banks. Often supplemented by constraint on interest rates, they give the central bank considerable control over bank behavior. However, control of the banks is not equivalent to controlling the financial sector. Since there are also other intermediaries, they may be expected to offset the direct effect of the regulation. Finally, he concluded (p.216) that the existence of nonblank intermediaries and the opportunity for banks to circumvent the regulations by active liability management, made the regulatory monetary policy less effective.

acquiring highly liquid assets, lending out cash balances for short periods. Banks lacking in reserves go out and acquire them from other banks excess reserves. Banks accommodate the corporate treasurers wish for a high liquid assets by inventing certificate of deposits (CDs) with a higher return. The firms paying on account pay the bills at the latest date possible. Some permit the payment period without penalty, tightening of collection procedures to make use of funds. Security dealers initiate repurchasing agreements whereby a customer can sell securities to the dealer for funds and agree to buy them back after a short time. The government agencies ease tight money conditions by selling some assets and backing payment for others, in general supporting some markets by easing the tightness of money. All these developments and others offset the tight money policy by increasing the velocity of money (McConnell and Brue, 1993, p.307).

16. The Monetary and Banking in Sudan

It is important to explain the development of money supply in Sudan and its major components, the Bank of Sudan monetary and credit policies and the problem of cash outflow from banking sector in Sudan. Finally, it presents the impact of that development on Sudan economy. Recently, in Sudan there were much debates among businessmen, politicians, economists, and even the public with regard to the impact of money on the economic activity in Sudan. Money and banking have integrated functions in achieving the socio-economic requirements. Osman Assayed (1998) assorted such major functions of money as medium of exchange, measure of value, store of value, and as future instrument of payments. He explained the primary banking services as deposits acceptance, expanding of credit, and discounting of commercial papers. Moreover, the secondary functions of banks include checks' clearance, exchanging of currencies, issuing of credit letters and gathering of savings from economic agents.

Modern economies as mentioned by Brunner and Meltzer (1990) and Maurer (2005) have multi-type of monetary system including three forms of money currency, coins, and nominal or deposits money. And banks, including the CB and Commercial banks in general, play a major role in monetary exchanges. The Commercial banks have the capability of multiplying the existing money, and their debts (claims) definitely play the role of money in the society. Conceptually, one of the CB essential tasks is to bring economic stabilization through controlling of rising prices via controlling the issuing and the flowing of money in the economy. Accordingly, commercial banks and the CB could be regarded as the backbone of modern monetary system (Assayed, 1998, p.272).

17.   Money Supply in Sudan

Money supply in Sudan is an essential macroeconomic variable denoted as broad money, M_2. Comprises of two main parts. The first part are means of current payment (M_1) that includes currency held by the public (circulated bank notes and coins) and demand deposits at banks, he second part of money supply is quasi-money that include local and deposits (BOS, 1998, annual report, 38th ed.). The main factors affecting money supply in Sudan sorted by the BOS are net foreign assets and valuation adjustment account. In addition to, net domestic assets, that is constituting claims on the public and private sectors. In addition to, the claims on specialized banks and other net claim items. Conversely, reserve money in Sudan is comprised of currency circulating outside the banking system, commercial banks balances held by the BOS, and other demand deposits (BOS, 1997, annual report, 37th ed.). The reserve money is regarded an extreme important item on the liability side of the bank of Sudan balance sheet. During the above mentioned period, the broad money supply in Sudan was increased. The periods 1972-1976 and 1976-1981 witnessed an increases in the broad money by 2.3 and 4% respectively. While the broad money supply through the period 1991-1995 increased by 14, reaching its highest level of growth - compared to its growth level of earlier 1970s.

Table (3) below shows the average growth rates of broad money supply in Sudan during different periods extending from 1972 to 2001. It indicates an increasing growth trend since the 1970s, continued through 1980s, and reaching its highest level at the mid of 1990s. After that the growth of broad money supply fell to a number of 30.1%.

Table (3) **Broad Money Supply Growth rates (in average) in Sudan**

Time periods	Average growth in Broad Money supply
1972-1976	23.3
1977-1981	32.9

1982-1986	38.5
1987-1991	46.8
1992-1996	90.98
1997-2001	30.1

Data Source: The Bank of Sudan

Table (3) below shows that the monetary growth of the first half of 1990s was associated with high growth rates in the nominal GDP. However, that growth in nominal GDP was also associated with high rates of inflation.

Table (3) **Growth Rates of Nominal GDP, M2, and Inflation in Sudan**

Years	M2 Growth rates	Nominal GDP Growth rates	The Rates of Inflation
1972	-	-	10.09
1973	0.19	0.18	16.02
1974	0.25	0.72	25.42
1975	0.14	-1.5	22.65
1976	0.28	0.15	1.70
1977	-1.90	0.27	17.18
1978	0.40	0.17	18.32
1979	0.25	0.15	33.91
1980	0.24	0.15	26.09
1981	0.22	0.23	22.56
1982	0.27	0.25	27.69
1983	0.22	0.20	13.13
1984	0.14	0.12	32.45
1985	0.47	0.28	46.33
1986	0.21	0.21	29.04
1987	0.26	0.46	24.98
1988	0.27	0.52	49.14

1989	0.37	0.21	74.08
1990	0.28	0.47	67.38
1991	0.40	0.53	122.52
1992	0.63	0.53	119.24
1993	0.47	0.51	101.18
1994	0.34	0.41	115.93
1995	0.43	0.28	68.97
1996	0.40	0.60	130.44
1997	0.93	0.36	47.19
1998	0.23	0.20	17.01
1999	o.20	0.19	16.16
2000	- 6.44	0.18	8.02
2001	0.20	0.12	4.92

Data Source: The Bank of Sudan

The table (2-3) below shows that in Sudan during the study period there was a high association between monetary growth and GDP growth. While the Rate of inflation showed less association with both the broad money and GDP growth rates.

Table (3-3) **Correlations between M2, Nominal GDP, and inflation rate in Sudan**

	m_t	gdp_t	inf_t
m_t	1.00	0.99	0.329
gdp_t	0.99	1.00	0.39
inf_t	0.329	0.39	1.00

Data Source: The Bank of Sudan

3.1.2. Factors affecting Money Supply in Sudan

The money supply (M2) is a fundamental macroeconomic variable in the Sudan. On the assets side of the Bank of Sudan balance sheet money supply is affected by various factors in Sudanese economy such as: changes in net domestic assets. That includes the borrowings from the banking system by the government and the public sector (Appendix 3, figure 3 diagram 4). Moreover, the money supply is influenced by the changes in net foreign assets, which in turn are affected by the changes in the foreign exchange rate. Finally, money supply is affected by changes in revaluation account which reflects the movements in the local counterpart of both foreign assets and liabilities of the Bank of Sudan balance sheet. That is a result of changes in the exchange rates of the Sudanese main currency the Pound against other currencies.

Table (3-4) **Money Supply Growth and Major Affecting Factors in Sudan**

Growth Rates	mt	gbt	Pbt	nfat	oex
Mt	1.00	-0.05	0.99	-0.05	0.16
Gbt	-0.05	1.00	-0.16	-0.15	-0.15
Pbt	0.99	-0.16	1.00	-0.05	0.23
Nfat	-0.06	-0.15	-0.05	1.00	-0.14
Oex	0.16	-0.15	0.23	-0.14	1.00

Data Source: The Bank of Sudan

Table (3-4) shows that the monetary growth in Sudan during the period 1972-2001 is much affected by the private sector borrowing than government borrowing. Official adjustments in the exchange rate have considerable association with broad money growth. Moreover, the monetary growth is weakly negative correlated to the growth in the net foreign assts. It is also noticeable the strong effect of private borrowing on monetary growth. However, there is a tradeoff between the growth in private borrowing and government borrowing. Osman Assayed (1998, p.280) indicated that for the period 1972-2001 public sector depends mainly on borrowing from the banking system to finance its rising expenditures. Considerable part of that borrowings were not directed to the targeted projects. The latter contributed nothing for the government budget. The effects of that borrowing are reflected as persistent increases in money supply.

Table (3-5) **Government Borrowing and Private Borrowing to broad money (M2)**

Year	Ratio Of GB/M2	Ratio of PB/M2
1972	0.77	na
1973	0.74	na
1974	0.72	na
1975	0.81	na
1976	1.02	na
1977	1.44	na

1978	1.1	0.52
1979	0.99	0.52
1980	0.91	0.5
1981	0.85	0.51
1982	0.56	0.54
1983	0.6	0.51
1984	1.02	0.51
1985	0.96	0.3
1986	0.68	0.35
1987	0.80	0.29
1988	0.81	0.25
1989	0.85	0.2
1990	0.79	0.25
1991	0.69	0.69
1992	0.57	na
1993	0.54	na
1994	0.44	na
1995	0.38	na
1996	0.43	na

1997	0.04	0.02
1998	0.04	0.02
1999	0.04	0.02
2000	0.37	0.21
2001	0.37	0.23

Data Source: The Bank of Sudan (calculated base on its data)

The main remarks on Table (3-5) below, indicates that during the period 1972-1975 the ratio of government borrowing was high. That could be attributed to the additional development expenditures on the public sector productive projects. Moreover, for the period 1976-1980 the ratio GB/M2 was even higher, nearly equal to the size of M2 . The main reason behind that is the decrease in external loans and foreign assistant. So, the government had to continue carrying the burden of financing its targeted productive projects, by increasing large budget deficits through borrowing from the banking system. Through 1980s decade, the ratio of GB/M2 exhibited at very high level, reflecting the increasing dependence of the government on the banking system. During the first half of the 1990s the ratio began to fall as a result of the tight monetary policies that aimed at lowering the inflationary deficit finance in order to attain economic stability. For the second half of the 1990s, the ratio of GB/M2 continued relatively at lower levels. However, for the two years of the twenty one century it witnessed high ratios of government borrowing relative to the wide money.

Reviewing the development in the government borrowing for the 1970s decade it is noticed that this period witnessed the first increases of budget deficits. Osman, A. Wahab (2000, p.162) indicated that the government was engaged in many productive projects. These projects financed by external short and medium term loans. However, these projects failed as a result of some difficulties. Accordingly, it failed in repaying that loans. To prevent these projects from failure, the government intended to finance through the budget. The large budget deficit in turn was covered by much borrowing from the banking system. Moreover, Osman, A. Wahab commented that the government borrowing from the banking system on average amounted to about LS 21 Milliard per month, adding to the increase in money supply. Thus, hyperinflation was aggravated.

During the 1980s decade the Sudanese economy was faced by many difficulties such as; natural catastrophes, political instability and lack of external debts and accumulation of its underpayments. Those events strongly contributed to the deterioration of the productive sector in Sudan. The statistics of that period showed large increases in the government borrowing from the banking system, presented an average annual increase of about 176.8% (Assayed, 1998).

Surveying the statistics of the government borrowing during the 1st half of 1990s, Assayed (1998, p.280) noted that by the end of 1995 it increased by about 13 compared to its size of 1990. So, he drew a conclusion that all available data figures about government borrowing from the banking system reflected much dependence of the central government and its entities on that source of finance. Explicitly, borrowings were neither directed to induce development, nor was it invested to generate revenues for the treasury and thus bring capabilities of repaying it. By looking through the above mentioned periods, it can be concluded that there was high growth in government borrowing from the banking system in Sudan. That could be regarded as one of the main factors influencing the money supply during that periods. Except for the years 1990 and 1995, in which, public sector borrowing was lowered while private borrowing from the banking system was expanded (Zavdji et al[29], 2000).

Private sector borrowing from the banking system in Sudan, could be regarded as one of the major factors affecting the money supply, M2. Such private borrowing, during the period1972-2001, was rapidly increasing (Table 3-6), thus raising the level of expenditures in the economy, pulling up of aggregate demand for goods and services. As for the period 1978-1989, private sector borrowing was increased by about 10 by the end of the period. It continued registering high increases in the 1990s, notably for the period 1992-1996 (Appendix 3, figure 3, diagram 3).

Table(3-6) **The Growth Rate of Private Borrowing from Banks**

---

[29] The Staff of IMF reported concerns with regard to the lack of private sector credit needed to finance economic growth. They supported the BOS policy of financial system liberalization that had taken place to date, including the removal of directed credit, has effectively revealed underlying weaknesses in the banking sector. Finally, they acknowledged the authorities that continuing structural problems such as laws which made loan collection difficult discouraged the extension of credit. Moreover, they outlined a program to reduce the cost and increase the availability of credit to the private sector.

Year	Growth of PB %	Year	Growth of PB %	Year	Growth of PB %
1972	0	1982	31.16	1992	-7468.3
1973	10	1983	17.5	1993	21.43
1974	11	1984	14.64	1994	23.74
1975	12	1985	9.63	1995	31.16
1976	12	1986	32.16	1996	17.5
1977	12	1987	10.44	1997	99.64
1978	100	1988	15.63	1998	11.29
1979	24.32	1989	20.76	1999	-1.88
1980	21.43	1990	42.09	2000	38.54
1981	23.74	1991	78.6	2001	29.32

Data Source: The Bank of Sudan

Table (3-4) shows unstable ratio of growth in the private borrowing from banking system through the three decades 1970s, 1980s, and 1990s. The 1970s decade witnessed low level of granting loans to the private sector by the banking system, because of the socialism tendency that affected setting of macro policies in Sudan at that time. However, that created bias towards public sector economic activities against the private sector.

Except for the year 1998, where the private borrowing grew at 100%.

During the 1980s decade, the growth of private borrowing exhibited some unstable behavior in response to the implemented economic policies, and it attained its highest level of growth (32%) in 1986.

At the beginning of the 1990s decade, namely, during the years 1990 and 1991, economic liberalization policies were adopted. And one of its important aims was to minimize the economic activities of the public sector and allow more opportunities for the private activities. A. Wahab (2000, p.68) explained that through the first year of economic liberalization, the Sudan witnessed government borrowing just to its planned ceiling. Adversely, the private sector borrowing from the banking system expanded largely, raising the money supply in the economy. During the period 1992-1994, growth rate of private sector borrowing fell in response to the constrained policies undertaken to combat hyperinflation associated with the economic liberalization process. As for the period 1995-1996 policy constraints were relaxed, in order to motivate economic growth in the face of mid-1990s recession. Accordingly, private sector borrowing grew from 18% in 1996 to 100% in 1997. In the same year the authorities introduced economic policy reforms, including monetary and fiscal policy reforms, aiming at bringing stability to the economy to combat unfavorable economic situations such as high rates of inflation and lower level of economic growth (A. Wahab, 2000). The years 1998-1999 represented an extension of medium term program of economic reform, in which the constraining policies continued aiming at more control of inflation rates, via targeting bringing down the growth rate the level of money supply (M2) to 24%. So, the growth rate of private borrowing were reduced to 11%. During 2000-2001 the private borrowing from the banking system witnessed some increases, so it registered growth at 38% and 29% respectively.

Foreign Assets in Sudan

The net foreign assets (NFA) is regarded as one of the Bank of Sudan's balance sheet items that reflects the position of foreign assets balance (Appendix 3, figure 3, diagram 4). Tight policies were implemented during the period 1970-1977. In that events, the exchange rate became administrative and motivate parallel and black market in foreign exchange dealing. During that period, there was large inflow of foreign source. That was exploited either to finance the development projects or to facilitate the foreign trade of Sudan. Facing that abnormal inflow of foreign financial resources, Sudan Council of Ministers authorized its ministers to arrange for financing their projects without referring to the Ministry of Finance (Osman, A. Wahab, 2000). The majority of these loans were either commercial short term loans or medium term ones, in addition to the cash loans for facilitating petroleum imports (about US $ 2, 654. 9 million). The projects financed at that time lacked solid feasibility studies and absorption capacity, so, they led to accumulation of foreign debts. The outcome of that process of foreign financial inflow at the end of 1977 could be summarized in the following two imbalances as noted by Osman, A. Wahab (2000, p.39 et seq.); the internal and external imbalances

1- The internal imbalance

The internal imbalance reflects that the current

expenditures in the Sudan exceeded its counterpart of revenues. These loans were used, mainly, for current consumption expenditures. Accordingly, a new law for financial and accounting procedures was issued by the Ministry of Finance in 1978.

2- The external imbalance

The process of borrowing from outside, unfortunately, lacked constitutional control. The commitment resulted in more pressures on the external account of Sudan balance of payments, showing much drawings, failure of repayments, and accumulation of foreign debts. So, the administration of these loans with their various forms was not proper. A memorandum demonstrated by the Minister of Finance in 1977 indicated that the external account on the BOS balance sheet amount to US $ 54.5 million in 1976. Add more, US $16 million was the expenditures on petroleum imports and embassies expenses. The total foreign debts on Sudan were about US $ 491.0 million. For the period 1978-1989 foreign assets in Sudan grew at negative rates, because of structural obstacles that caused deterioration of 46% in Sudan's exports (Osman, A. Wahab ,2000). That period also witnessed negative inflows of foreign aids and foreign loans. Those negative inflows could be interpreted by two points of view.

First, it is indicated for the failure of public investment in Sudan to make full-exploitation of foreign financial sources. Therefore, there were less produced outlet to the Treasury. Thus, these events led to an accumulation of foreign debt to the extent that it had been rescheduled by Paris and London clubs. The foreign debt in 1984 was US $ 6 milliard and enlarged to be US $ 13.9 milliard in

1990. Through the 1980s decade the ratio of foreign debt to the nominal GDP rose to 110% and the ratio of underpayments to the exports revenues rose to 600%. The final impact of that event was a reduction in the ratio of investment to the nominal GDP from 22% in 1980 to 10% in 1990.

Secondly, that negative inflow in the foreign debt could be interpreted from another angel, that the second half of the 1980s witnessed the collapse of Eastern Europe and Soviet Union Socialistic Republics. That declared the end of the hot competition between the East and West camps to attract the developing countries. Thus, their assistant and loans to that countries were decreased.

18.   The Banking System in Sudan

Bankers' activities in Sudan, as in many developing countries started by opening branches of foreign banks. While modern banks in Sudan were introduced at the beginning of the 20th century, namely, by the establishment of the National Bank of Egypt branch of Khartoum. For almost 50 years, until 1949, the only other bank operating was Barclays Bank which was established in 1913. During the period 1949-1960, seven banks were established in order to provide services to the commercial sector registered as private companies (Table 3-5). As in many developing countries, bankers activities started by opening branches of foreign banks.

Table (3-7) **Foreign Banks in Sudan (1949 – 1960)**

Mother country of the bank	The bank
Egypt	National Bank of Egypt
England	Bank of Barclays D.C.O.
Turkey	Ottoman Bank
France	Lyonnais Bank of Credit
Jordan	The Arab Bank
Egypt	The Bank of Egypt
Ethiopia	National Bank of Ethiopia

Source: Sudan Year book, 1983

Bank of Sudan and the Banking System[30]

The Ministry of Finance and Economic Affairs was responsible for monitoring and controlling the commercial banks activities. Whereas, the *Currency Board created* in 1956 was in charge of issuing currency. In 1959 announced for setting of the BOS, that actually, started working in 1960. Carrying out the previous mentioned functions. The BOS hold three *essential tasks*; as banker of banks, regulates credit and monetary process, and to facilitate investment and external trade. Saeed (2004) sorted out the main functions of the BOS.

---

[30] Figure 2, appendix 3.

That the BOS is responsible for money issuing (paper and coins), keeping government and public entities accounts and to administrate the internal and external debts. In addition to its responsibility to set the monetary policy, developing researches and planning the development of the banking system. Adding to its essential tasks. Before 1984, as mentioned by Magzoub (2000, p.26) the BOS used various monetary policy instruments to directly control credit. Besides, it was controlling money supply via interest rates and changing cash reserves ratios. As well the BOS controlled credit through credit ceilings. Recently, the BOS implemented certain amendment to the 1993 and the 2002 new law of the BOS. Concerning banks Islamization, the BOS played a central role to be implemented to all banking system. Finally, the BOS adopted a monetary policy consistent with aims of the national comprehensive strategy.

Commercial Banks[31] activity in Sudan started in 1960, its ownership and activities were dominated by foreigners, and afterward, a six new banks were followed. The main features of commercial banks at that time were external trade finance and its services were urban-concentrated.

Nationalization of commercial banks in Sudan was stated in 1970s, in the context of stated nationalization policy of foreign institutions and companies. That was in accordance with prevailed socialism principles at that

---

[31] Figure 2, appendix 3.

time. That policy made the BOS the sole owner of the commercial banks and gave it full administrative control, as well as discretionary power over their commercial transactions. These banks were renamed and subsequently were regrouped into four groups (Table 3-8). Due to contradictions between the 1970 decree and the 1925 Companies Act, there was a lot of ambiguity in the relationship between the commercial banks and the BOS. That situation was solved in 1973 by enacting of the Savings and Investment Act. The commercial banks were regarded as independent public corporations. Moreover, a board was initiated to monitor the activities of these banks. The highest repercussion of that decision was that the BOS was deprived of an important means of controlling the creation of money, credit facilities, and foreign dealings (Sudan Yearbook, 1983).

After two years of dealing with nationalized banks, the government decided to repeal the Savings and Investment Act, and to give the BOS more effective control. That amendment made both the BOS and Ministry of Finance and Economic Planning owners of the banks. Moreover, the BOS retained full control over commercial banks activities.

Table (3-8) **Nationalized Banks in Sudan in the 1970s**

The foreign bank	Nationalized to:
Barclays Bank D. CO.	The State Bank for Foreign Trade
National Bank of Egypt	National Ommdurman Bank
The Arab Bank Co. Ltd.	Red Sea Commercial Bank
Bank of Egypt	National Co-operative Bank
Lyonnais Bank of Credit	Elneilein Bank

Source: Sudan now, Sudan Year Book, 1983

Magzoub (2000, p.24) showed the main purposes of the nationalization policy at that time were as follows: (1) strengthening the balance of payments. (2) export promotion and increasing its returns. (3) Attracting remittances of Sudanese working abroad. (4) enhancing competition among local banks to improve their services in rural and remote areas. (5) improving banking technology. (6) removing of foreign banks domination over the national capital resources. (7) motivation of the local banking system to play its role of financial intermediation. (8) Direct control of the BOS over the monetary process. (9) Rid off the capitalistic monopolies.

Evaluating nationalization policy to banks in Sudan, Saeed (2004, p.46) Summarized its advantages to include nationalizing banking services, getting benefits of external facilities and redistributing banks finance among diversified economic activities. Moreover, private banks deposits in general witnessed large expansion; reflecting the increased confidence in banking system. Then again, nationalization of banking system enabled the monetary authorities in Sudan to achieve the stated goals of bank credit policy. Finally, nationalization of banking system in Sudan encouraged banks to spread all over the country. Also, it enabled the BOS to initiate a special balance sheet for the foreign exchange. On the other hand, Saeed (2004, p.48) sorted out main disadvantages of banks nationalization in Sudan mentioned the large loss in the convenience of stockholders and private depositors, especially, the foreigners towards banking activities in Sudan. Moreover, commercial banks resistance in opposition to the BOS constraints weakened the control role the BOS over the banking system. As a result, there was lack in banks' finance to private investment and rural activities. Furthermore, foreign companies intended to reduce its exports from Sudan, that matter, negatively, affected Sudan's foreign reserves position.

After the nationalization of commercial banks in 1970, an open door policy towards *foreign* and *joint venture banks*[32] has been licensed and commenced operations. Some foreign banks such as the *Islamic Banks*, The

---

[32] Figure 2, appendix 3.

National Development Bank, the Islamic Co-operative Bank, and four foreign banks were permitted to work in Sudan. Moreover, banking regulations permitted less capital requirement so as to make funds more available for banks to expand loans to economic sectors (Sudan Year Book, 1983, p.120).

Specialized Banks were banks specialized as development banks to provide credit facilities to their respective sectors(Table 3-9). To enable the specialized banks to play their developmental role their capital were rose. In adherence to Islamic Law, the government decided to abolish usury in the provision of credit facilities to the customers of these banks (Sudan Year Book, 1983, p. 120).

Table (3-9) **The first specialized banks in Sudan**

The bank	Setting year	initial capital
Sudanese Agricultural Bank	1957	£S 7 millions
Sudanese Estates Bank	1961	£S 7 millions
Sudanese Industrial Bank	1961	£S 7 millions raised to £S 10 millions in 1966

Sudanese Savings Bank	1973	

Source: Sudan now, Sudan Year Book, 1983

As an alternative mean of charging these services, a fixed charge based on each specialized bank's overhead and operational costs been considered. The main problem with that approach was its high per unit cost. Another important development of banking organization in Sudan was the initiation of *Sudanese Development Corporation*[33] SDC, which was established in 1974 by an initial capital £S 500 millions. The SDC was an independent organization, with foreign reserves kept abroad without interference of any sort from the BOS. It provided credit facilities for a wide array of developmental projects, preferring joint venture-projects with the central government, other public corporations, foreign or local companies and technical assistance organizations.

Rural Development Corporations were bodies created to facilitate rural projects in collaboration with regional governments. The BOS had no power over that bodies except for that period 1973-1975. Meantime, the BOS exercised full control over commercial banks. However, the BOS had more power to control specialized banks such as Agricultural, Industrial, and Estates Banks, because of the financial problems faced that banks at

---

[33] Figure 2, appendix 3.

that time (Sudan now, Sudan Year Book, 1983, p.120).

19.   The Islamization of Banking in Sudan

Islamization of the Banking System in Sudan aimed at providing Islamic non-interest dealings instead of the dominating interest dealings. For that purpose Islamic banks were first initiated in Sudan. The *Islamic banks* differ from their traditional counterparts in the conceptual framework and commitments. As noted by Awad, M. H. (1995, P.1) the Islamic banks aimed at Islamization of the entire economy ... has a fundamental global massage to make radical changes in the international financial system. Those changes could be attainable through the interactions among Islamization elements including the banking dynamic factors. Awad, M. H. (1995, p.7) also argued that a country like Sudan, with a considerable number of Islamic Banks, the *process of banks Islamization* is expected to go on much more than any other country. Here a National Islamic Strategy is required to enable those banks to play their economic role. The remark here, Islamic finance was not a first trial in Sudan. In the 1930s decade Abdurrahman Elmahdi had set Islamic regulations to finance the irrigated-cotton projects of White Nile (Mekki – Riyadh – Shawal). Awad, M. H. (1995) also summarized the rationales behind Islamic banks initiation in Sudan in points as follows:

1- Islamic banks in Sudan have good portfolio balance, as a result they gained much internal and external support.
2- The financial consolidation between Sudanese and foreign Islamic banks is much easy.
3- The ex-1984 period non-Islamic situations is impossible now to prevail.
4- Much efforts had been exerted to attract foreign resources and remittances of Sudanese working abroad.

Islamization process in Sudan started with the introduction of Sharia Law, which replaced the former civil code. In the economic field, it outlawed the use of interest rates in financial transactions that created major problems to the banking sector. It was already in process through the formation of a number of Islamic banks, which successfully, introduced a ***system of participatory financing*** of business transactions. However, the government decided that charging interest would became illegal and that interest payment claims would be unrecoverable through the courts. However, even after that decision, some of commercial banks continued charging interest. The government asked bankers' committee to submit concrete proposals on how the country could proceed with further Islamization of the banking system, a year after the legislation was passed (the World Bank, 1983, p.52).

During 1983, five new banks were licensed and authorized for commercial banking business in Sudan; (1) National bank for Export and Import, (2) Blue Nile

Bank Ltd., (3) Tadamon Islamic Bank, (4) Sudanese Islamic Bank and (5) Islamic Co-operative Bank. In addition to that, branches were opened of sixteen commercial banks to further banking services in the country. Moreover, Western Sudan Islamic Bank and Baraka Islamic Bank started in the 1984 (Bank of Sudan Annual Report, 24, 1983).

The traditional system of interest dealings was abolished. Meanwhile, Islamic dealings promulgated to the banking system in Sudan. Some problems associated the banking system Islamization were pointed out by Ahmed, S. M. (2000, p.23-25) as follows:

1. Some banks lack access to apply, properly, the Islamic principle of dealings. Therefore, that led to much form of illusionary murabaha, under repayment of bank loans because of the high margins of profits that were set by banks.
2. Weak control by the BOS over the banks, where policy focus on passing of managerial decisions, imposing of penalties and consolidation policy ... etc.
3. Banks showed strong tendency to own large estates, which affect their liquidity position.
4. Banks Situation Conformity project had threatened the majority of banks through *liquidation procedures*.
5. The declared banking policy resulted in opening numerous branches that competed in a limited narrow banking market. This hindered banking spread, thus, weakened the rural development.

In brief, Ahmed S. M. (2000, p. 26) concluded his notion

that implementation of Islamic principle in the banking system in Sudan was faced by some limitations. The main cause behind that limitations was the lack of full awareness about practicing the Islamic principles of dealings in banks. As a result there were much serious improper practices of Islamic principles of dealings, failure of bank loans repayments, increasing of the cash outflow from the banking system. in addition to the spread of income inequality among diverse groups of the society. Furthermore, geographical spread of banks all over the country affect negatively, banks efficiency. Finally, some banks suffered by losses; that event justified the introduction of banking reforms policy by the BOS. The program which aimed at raising the banks capital efficiency through several procedures.

Banking System Conformity (BSC)

According to the law of banking in Sudan of 1991, it was decided that banks have to reform their set up within a three years period, starting from July 1994.

The main objectives of the program as reported by the Centre of Strategic Studies (1998, p.180) were included in four reforms:

1- Financial Reform

Including a group of steps:

a.   Capital and reserves adequacy, that indicated that all Sudanese banks have to accommodate their banking set up according to the main principles of Basel Committee. Moreover, the BOS set a program for every individual banks to realize the required percentage of capital adequacy.

b.   Management and adequacy of banks liquidity.

c.   Guarantee of best exploitation of banks resources.

d.   Setting up of unique system for debt classification.

e.   Attainment of minimum level of risk concerning investment and finance by banks.

2- Managerial Reform

Its main procedures included the following:

a.   Banks have to set clear-cut borders for their financial and managerial powers, authorities, and responsibilities. Moreover, they must maintain efficiency measures and improve their system of making decisions.

b.   Proceeding of internal auditing and its direct supervision by the board of directors.

c.   A body of legislative control was promulgated to ensure good application of Islamic codes by the commercial banks.

d.   Concerning the appointing and reappointment of the board of directors and general managers, priory consent from the BOS must be obtained.

e.   The banking system in Sudan must exert more efforts to for promote and diversify banking services adequacy.

3- Technical Reform

1. Unification of the terminologies and accounting system. Accordingly, banks must implement the

Financial Accounting Act instructions for the banks, financial and Islamic institutions.
2. Banks have to develop their internal control system.
3. Updating of data collection and data analyzing methods.
4. Updating of the decision making system and the follow up process.
5. Training.
6. Inspection and internal auditing supported with well qualified and well trained members.
4- Legal reform

a.   Changing of both banks and financial institutions into public subscription companies.
b.   Revising of contracts and establishment rules, according to the declared policy, the project of Banking System Conformity and the Banking Regulation of 1991 law.
Banks in 1994 were classified into two main groups (the Centre of Strategic Studies 1998, p.181):

a.   Banks who conformed their situation by 100% .
b.   Banks who conformed their position in most required items. Banks need more wide conformation, concerning these, some measures were imposed to carryon the reforms, such as capitalization of profits, raising authorized and paid-up capital, liquidation of some fixed assets and stock investment. Finally, measure of lowering expenses and increasing revenues could be operated. The banks included here were those who failed to provide enough required information about their position.
The banking conformity project was incomplete by the end of 1997.

With regard to the *Policy Reform* of the 1990s in the Banking system in Sudan. Saeed (2000, p.31-32) argued that the main objectives of this reform was to enhance the effectiveness and adequacy of the Sudanese banks. Moreover, the policy intended to activate the role of banks in the economy through during the transitional stage of the economy from a controlled economy to an open free economy. Accordingly, he sorted out *the main procedures of the initial reforms* as follows:

1. In 1990, banks in Sudan were permitted to initiate and open branches all over the urban and rural areas in Sudan, a phenomenon known as banking spread policy.
2. In 1992, currency exchange rate and major prices of goods and services were liberalized. Moreover, to motivate investment the administrative constraints on foreign exchange dealings were lowered.
3. In 1994, the system of credit ceilings was repealed to enable banks to devote their credit resources to the various sectors and activities in the economy.
4. Also in 1994, the project of Banking System conformity was stated, to be carried out within three-year period. This was intended to update Sudanese banks to the recent developments in banking and capital adequacy criteria adopted worldwide.
5. In 1995, a clearing house for foreign exchange was established in the BOS. That procedures facilitated the transactions and settlement of payments in accordance to its specified laws and rules, instead of making settlements via foreign correspondents. Moreover, foreign exchange companies were

permitted to deal in foreign currencies. The aim of such policy was to add more flexibility to foreign exchange dealings of the private sector.

6. Also in 1995, the Khartoum Stock of Exchange (KSE) was initiated to activate and develop dealings in financial stocks.

7. In 1996, the Corporation of Banks Deposits Guarantee Fund started. Its main task was to lower the financial risks in banks.

8. A control system was suggested to regulate banking transactions and to grantee their satisfaction capital requirements. The rationale behind was to reduce the unforeseen risks and strengthen banks' capabilities in the face recession.

9. As an indirect control instrument, the legal reserve system was implemented. Moreover, banks which failed to maintain that requirement could face liquidation procedures.

10. During the period 1998-1999, structural reforms were implemented to the banks in order to protect and raise their net worth to the maximum possible level.

11. In 1999, a daily room for transactions in foreign exchanges was initiated. Accordingly, the exchange rate became determined through market mechanism.

12. Also in 1999, regulations and orientations were implemented to allow banks to accept the Islamic Measures of Accounting and Auditing. Moreover, strict rules of transparency were to be followed.

13. To support the reforms policies, the Sudan Company for Financial Services was initiated. One of its tasks was to issue and sell Musharaka Certificates of the BOS (CMCs), that was issued to meet certain commercial banks assets. The CMCs are held by both

the BOS and Ministry of Finance. While, issuing of Shahama Certificates (GMCs) based on government shares in some public institutions. Both, certificates enabled their holders to gain some returns after a certain time (Mohamed Khare, 2000, p.75-83).

The evaluation of the first banking reforms in Sudan showed that banks have gained advantages of permission and activation to spread its branches from 493 in 1991 to 695 in 1997. In addition by liberalization of exchange rate, the parallel market vanished. Moreover, they benefit from repealing of credit ceilings and developing of financial stock dealings. The events that created some sort of diversity in contents of the banks investments. The matter enabled them to control their liquidity. Unfortunately, the liberalization of exchange rate devaluated banks' assets. Furthermore, banks continued on granting loans, only, to their traditional dealers. Therefore, banks committed biases towards their depositors against the investors in granting loans. Moreover, the reforms scored less and limited effects on Sudan economy because, of the continuation of the administrative constraints on the market economy. Some banks accounts were at the BOS exposure. So, they were exposed to some penalties. While another group emerged structural disequilibria and failed to fulfill the program requirements, so, it was liquidated (Sudan IMF Staff Report No.00/70).

The second banking reforms of the period (2000-2002) were implemented in the framework of Structural

Adjustment Policy SAP. Its main objective in the field of banks was to strengthen the solvency of the banking system in Sudan. Thus, supporting banks financial position and activate its social and developmental role. The main policy decisions were:

1. Banks Amalgamation: It was selective decision, carried on under supervision of the BOS for technical assistance - the selected number of groups was six.

2. Establishment of minimum level paid-in-capital[34] at SD. 3 billion, the level that satisfied requirements of financial solvency. Therefore, banks were obligated to meet that condition in three parts within three years, starting from the first year of the reform.

3. The public commercial banks amalgamation. The decision aimed at raising its capital to the minimum level requirement with consultancy of the Ministry of Finance and National economy.

4. Stating of detailed policy, concerning the specialized banks with consultancy of the ministry.

5. Reprocessing of underpayments of banks finance, for that a body was created including the BOS, Ministry of Finance, and the corporation of Deposits Guarantee fund.

---

[34] With regard to enhance the bank soundness key to achieve macroeconomic objectives. The BOS works with banks on measures to reduce the size of non-performing loans and consider for raising provisioning requirements to ensure sufficient coverage of doubtful loans. Moreover, announced plans have to be set to assure banks' compliance with an appropriate capital adequacy ratio, including the introduction of incentives and penalties for non-compliant banks. Given the tasks above, IMF Staff expect the BOS also to include some consolidation of banks, as further long-term technical assistant is requested from the Fund in the area of bank restructuring,

6. The BOS declared incentives and privileges for banks who achieve the targets of the reform such as reprocessing of underpayment of loans and restructuring of the bank.

7. some procedures were imposed to those banks who failed to meet the requirements of conformity program, or failed to fulfill the required minimum level of capital. So, financial and administrative punishments were levied.

The Model Specification

We describe how the model equations were specified, the model was formulated then the data was assessed and its sources. Finally the empirical results were presented and some analytical comments were made.

Model Equations

The aim of constructing the model system is to measure the impact of cash outflow from the banking sector on major macroeconomic variables in Sudan.

Effective Liquidity Function

Consider a simple monetary economy, the real output process is exogenously given. After the production of good and financial services, economic agents choose their real money holdings according to the availability of banks loans as following:

$$EL_t = P \cdot zBL_t \underline{\hspace{3cm}} (1)$$

On the left hand side, (EL_t) is nominal effective liquidity measured as the demand for nominal money balances as perceived by the central bank, consists of cash held by the public and demand deposits. The right hand side term ($P \cdot zBL_t$), is a nominal proportion (z) of bank loans (BL_t) that individuals prefer to hold as liquid money balances. Many economists such as Brunner and Meltzer (1990, p.371) and Maurer (2005, p.21) to day believe that lending is a crucial item on the assets side of the bank balance sheet and significantly influences economic activity. Dornbusch (1990, p.598) emphasized this direction preferring credit view to money one: *the credit view asserts that money created through bank loans has a higher velocity than does money created through bank security purchases. This follow the fact that individuals and firms that takeout bank loans are more likely to spread the proceeds on goods and services than... those... selling securities to the banks. Hence, ... aggregate expenditures will be stimulated strongly by an increase in bank lending than by an equal increase in bank securities purchases.* Dornbusch and Fischer (1990, p.396) argued that people are interested in purchasing power of their money holdings, i.e., the value of their cash balances in terms of goods the cash will buy. They described the concept of real liquid balances as follows: *an individual is free from money illusion, if a change in the level of prices, holding all real variables constant, leaves the person's real behavior, including real money demand unchanged*". Accordingly, EL_t is expected to increase as the prices level (P_t) increases. As well as the bank loans (BL_t) with demand for nominal money balances (EL_t).

20. Money Supply Function

According to Choi and Seonghwan (2000, p.5) money supply (M_t) is governed by the following rule:

$$M_t = P_t (Y_t)^{\alpha} (EL_t/P_t)^{\alpha-1} e^{\rho Ht} _____(1)$$

Where P_t is the central bank's presumed price level, Y_t is real GDP trend consistent with long-run output, EL_t/P_t is real money demand perceived by the central bank, H_t is policy stance following a stationary process with zero mean, α, α-1, are elasticities of money supply (M_t) with respect to the trend and real money demand, respectively. Assuming that Mt is neither fully endogenous nor fully exogenous (0 < α < 1). Rule (1) composes of a trend component (Y_t) reflecting a Freidman-type of money growth similar to that in Ramey (1993, p. 245 et seq.) or Good friend (1997) in that it supports prices rigidity. Judd and Taylor (1998, p.2-16) explain that the CB follows a kind of a rule which suggests that the CB should increase the interest rate resulting in a decrease in M_t, that is, if inflation rises above a target or if output is above its trend. Similarly, then, Taylor policy rule (1) requires a tightening policy with respect to higher inflation and a loosening policy with respect to larger long-term output. Here rule (1) does not require increasing an interest rate as output exceeds its trend since the output process is endowment determined. Meanwhile, it is extended to reflect a tighter policy stance in response to higher output growth to reduce M_t (Choi and Seonghwan, 2000, p.6).

21.   Money Demand Function

Money Demand Function is characterized as a choice between alternative real and financial assets available to economic agents. Pinōn-Farah (1998, p.7) specified the money real balances within a portfolio framework as a function of wealth to comprise money, real domestic assets, and domestic and financial assets. He modified the standard model of the monetary sector as originally developed by Branson (1977, p.69 et seq.) which yields an equation as follows:

$$(M/P)_t = \beta_0 + \beta_1 DevY_t + \beta_2 W_t + \beta_3\, i(Oex^e, i_f)_t + \beta_4 i + \beta_5\, Inf_t^e \quad (3)$$
$$\beta_0, \beta_1\, \beta_2 > 0,\ \beta_{31} < 0,\ \beta_{32} = 0, \beta_4 < 0,\ \beta_5 = 0$$

Where

$(M/P)_t$ Is real money balances

$DevY_t$ is real output gap which represents deviations of real output from its potential level, included to capture the impact of economic cycle on the model system variables.

W_t is nominal wealth and proxies by quasi money, QM_t.

oex_t^e is expected depreciation of domestic currency.

i_f is foreign interest rate.

i is domestic nominal interest rate.

INF_t^e is expected inflation rate.

The above equation expressed that the allocation of wealth to money balances depends on the level of demand for transactions (Y_t) and the opportunity cost of holding domestic money i.e. expected yield of competing assets. The expected inflation rate (INF_t) and domestic interest rate (i) are intended to represent the opportunity costs with respect to holding physical assets and domestic financial assets, as well as the expected yield on domestic investment. Expected yields on foreign assets, include the level of foreign interest rates (i_f) and expected rate of depreciation of domestic currency, OEX_t^e (Pinōn-Farah, 1998, p.7).

To examine how the policy stance causes deviations from long-run money demand relationship, Choi and Seonghwan Oh, 2000, p.12). Estimated percentage deviations were regressed from long-run equilibrium Values on the intercept and policy stance measure (policy shock):

$$\hat{U}_t = \rho_0 + \rho_1 H_t + E_t \qquad \rho_1 > 0$$

Where:

$\hat{u}_t$ is estimated residual of equation, (3) multiplied by 100 and H_t a policy stance measure. well-established indicators are used as instrumental variables (IV). Such instrument sets include {intercept, high-powered money, and non-borrowed reserves} and {intercept, changes in the discount rate, and the changes in non-borrowed reserves}. Since the error term in equation (3) may involve strong persistence due to the partial adjustment of money holdings, assume that E_t is serially correlated. The estimated coefficient of the policy stance, ρ_1 was positive, but insignificant, and the generalized R^2 that was proposed by Pesaran and Smith (1994) as an appropriate measure of fit for IV regression, is small. Choi and Seonghwan found a little evidence of the effect of the money supply factor on money demand for their whole sample.

Cost of Resources Adjustment

Cost adjustment (DM_t) occurs when money holdings $(M/P)_t$ differ from the money supply (Mt). The cost function is to be assumed symmetric for simplicity:

$$dM_t = \Gamma_0 + \Gamma_1 (RMB - M)_t \qquad (4)$$

Where, $\Gamma_1 > 0$ is a cost parameter. Choi and Seonghwan

(2000, p.8) noted that a change in money holdings in the period t induces a change in money supply, which, however, may not accommodate fully the change in money demand. Discrepancies between $(RMB)_t$ and $(M)_t$ generate an adjustment cost that reflects real resources spent for the reallocation to match the money holdings with the money stock available.

Aggregate Demand Function

To specify the aggregate demand, concern the neoclassical formula mentioned by Dornbusch and Fischer (1990, p.545) through joining the goods market equilibrium and assets market equilibrium to obtain the aggregate demand level. That could be determined by autonomous spending, real money balances, and expected rate of inflation. All mentioned determinants are positively related to aggregate demand. It follows that the change in aggregate demand is determined by the changes in autonomous spending, real balances, and the expected rate of inflation. Assuming that the only change in autonomous spending comes from fiscal policy change, which represents the changes in output and budget deficit. Accordingly, aggregate demand's function is written as:

$$\Delta AD_t = (AD_t - AD_{t-1}) = f\ (dM_t, V2_t, BD_t)$$

then:

$$AD_t = \Delta_1 AD_{t-1} + \Delta_2 dM_t + \Delta_3 V2_t + \Delta_4 BD_t, \quad \Delta_1, \Delta_2, \Delta_3, \Delta_4 > 0 \quad (5)$$

Where:

AD   is current aggregate demand and Δ denotes for the change in aggregate demand.

AD_{t-1} is previous aggregate demand.

dM_t is cost adjustment that reflects real resources spent for the reallocation to match the money holdings with the money stock available or the changes in money balances, is expected to be positive (increases). That is when real balance holdings exceed the available money stock and the reverse is true.

V_{2t} is velocity of money to capture effect of rises in real transaction relative to the available stock of money.

BD   is budget deficit to capture the fiscal policy change.

Aggregate Supply Function

Dornbusch and Fischer (1990, p.714) noted that the aggregate supply function is of a Cobb-Douglass formula which links the amount of produced output (Y) of the economy to its inputs of factors of production, the amount of labor force (N), the amount of capital (K), and the state of technical knowledge (A):

$$Y_t = A \ (N_t)^{1-E} \ (K_t)^{\ E}, \qquad\qquad E > 0 \qquad\qquad (6)$$

According to Jones and Scrimgeour (2005, p.3) the above equation is a neoclassical growth model production function in equation (6) satisfies the standard neoclassical properties which are constant returns to scale positive diminishing marginal products of both capital and labor (Jones 2004).

22.   Capital Stock

The capital stock represents the accumulation of past investment. Supply side supporters such as Baskin (1988), presents how created taxation system discriminates strongly against savers: *if savers receive a lower rate of return as result of taxation, they reduce savings, and therefore, capital accumulation is reduced.* Thus the growth of the capital stock requires to increase saving or reduce budget Deficits. To explain such point of view, Dornbusch and Fischer (1990, p.723) emphasizes the links between saving and investment. Recall the Keynesian equilibrium condition when the goods market is cleared and net exports are zero, then investment minus saving equals the budget surplus, or:

$$Iv_t - S_t = (T - G)_t$$

$$S_t = Iv_t - (G - T)_t$$

The initial time of capital accumulation depends on a certain amount of available private saving as an initial capital or:

$$K_t = \int S_0 \cdot dt$$

Accordingly:

$$K_t = \varphi_1 Iv_t + \varphi_2 (BD)_t, \quad \varphi_1 > 0, \varphi_2 < 0 \qquad (7)$$

Where K_t is the capital in the period (t). It is proxied by the supply of private savings (S_t). Accordingly, the capital (K_t) increases when investment (Iv_t) is higher and budget deficit (BD)$_t$ is smaller (Dornbusch and Fischer, 1990, p.725). The first term of equation (7) of capital accumulation, assumes that all investment as undertaken by the private sector gives incentives with government fiscal investment regulations. The second term shows how budget deficits, have strong adverse effects on long-term growth. Moreover, budget deficits imply a reduction in full-employment output growth. Therefore, Kotiff (1984) emphasized that funds are diverted from growth toward other purposes i.e., there is a tradeoff between growth and the social objectives that may lie behind a budget deficit.

23.   Investment Demand Function

The investment function depends on the gradual adjustment hypothesis: in a flexible way with a generalized form of an older accelerator model of investment. According to Bernanke (1983) this hypothesis postulates the investment as proportional to the changes in the level of GDP. Its rationale is that the larger the gap between the existing and the desired capital stocks, the more rapid is a firm's rate of investment. It assumes that the firm plans to close a fraction of the gap (g) each period. Therefore, the gradual formulation of the amount of net investment at the end of the period will be:

$$Iv_t = g(K^* - K_t)$$

Where g is speed of adjustment of K_t to K^*, the larger is g, the faster the gap is reduced. Thus the factors that increase K^* increase the rate of investment. Therefore, an increase in expected output, a reduction in the real rate of interest, or an increase in the investment tax credit will each increase the rate of investment.

Dornbusch and Fischer (1990, p.319) based on accelerator model of investment, derived some dynamic behavioral aspects concerning investment. They argued that there are two sources of dynamic behaviors. The first arises from expectations, because, K* depends on the firm's estimate of future permanent output as a weighted average of past output level. There will be lags in the adjustment of the actual level of output and the level of permanent output: $I_t = j\,Dev\,(PY)_t$

Where, j is a constant representing the ratio of change in the desired capital stock to the change in real output. This relation creates the potential for investment spending to fluctuate a good deal. Thus, investment is expected to be proportional to the changes in the output. Then when the economy is in a state of recovery, I_t will be positive. In addition, when it is in a recession, I_t will be negative. However, the accelerator model predicts that I_t will fluctuate considerably the future.

The second dynamic behavior of I_t arises from adjustment lags. Firms plan to close only a proportion of the gap between actual and desired capital stocks each period, so, the adjustment lags produce lagged response of investment to changes in the variables[35] that affect the desired capital stock. However, the model in practice is not a complete model of investment. Because, it ignores the costs of capital[36] as a financial determinant of investment decision, the cases of credit rationing, and

---

[35] The research suggest those variables to be the private saving and the general price index.
[36] For recent development concerning the model of financial accelerator with risk premium see Elekdag et al (2005, pp.3-4).

the impact of current profits. Finally, the investment function will take the following specification form:

$$Iv_t = \Omega_1 K^*_{t-1}(P_t, S_t) + \Omega_2 \, DevY_t, \quad \Omega_{11} > 0, \Omega_{12} > 0, \Omega_2 > 0 \quad (8)$$

Where:

DevY$_t$ Deviations of the actual real output from its permanent level

The Rate of Inflation

Barrel et al (1997, p.38) practiced the Taylor rule on a simple reduced model that could leave the price level indeterminate, in the sense that it depends upon the parameters of the model and not on target nominal variable:

$$INF_t = \Lambda_1(IINF)_{t-1} + \Lambda_2(OEX)_{t-1} + \Lambda_3(RM\,B)_{t-1} + \Lambda_4 e_{1t-1} + e_{2t},$$
$$\Lambda_1, \; \Lambda_2, \; \Lambda_4 > 0, \Lambda_3 < 0$$

Where (INF) $_{t-1}$ is in a previous period of inflation, this supports the hypothesis that expectations are adaptive i.e. people based on the past behavior of inflation. Thus under adaptive expectations the rate of inflation expected for next year might be the rate of inflation of last year (Dornbusch and Fischer, 1990, p.521). Rational expectations hypothesis implies that people do not make systematic mistakes in forming their expectations. On average according to rational expectations hypothesis, it is correct because people understand the environment in which they operate. $(OEX)_{t-1}$ is price level reflecting the depreciation rate of domestic currency and $(RMB)_{t-1}$ is nominal or money wealth (Barrel et al, 1999, p.38). e_{1t-1} is serially un-correlated error.

Bank Loans

Banks determine loans in response to monetary authorities' decisions with respect to reserve requirements, by holding excess reserves in the face of tight monetary policy:

"*When the Fed tightens monetary policy, banks respond by tightening their credit standards. As a result many smaller firms are cut off from funds, rather than rationing the limited amount of funds through market forces by allowing interest rates to move up to make clearing level ...etc*". (Lloyd, 1997, p.591). Banks reserves R_t can be broken into two components required reserves $(RR)_t$ and excess reserves $(ER)_t$ as follows:

$$R_t = (RR)_t + (ER)_t$$

Assume that banks adjust their actual holdings of excess reserves to the desired amounts instantaneously. Then excess reserves are difference between banks' reserves and required reserves:

$$(ER)_t = R_t - (RR)_t$$

The reserve requirements is a certain proportion (r) of banks deposits, D_t, specified by the CB as follows:

$$(RR)_t = r \cdot D_t$$

According to the money view[37] a tightened monetary policy will directly influence economic activity, regardless the channel. Meanwhile, lending or credit view[38] believes that lending is a crucial item on the asset side of banks balance sheet. Moreover, it affects the GDP above and beyond the role of money (Lloyd, 1997, p.598). Furthermore, Lloyd (1997, p.108) argued that, for pre-1980 budget deficits, most economists such as Tobin (1983, p.201, et seq.) agreed that a larger budget deficit may arouse inflation, thereby pulling interest rates via the Fisher effect. He advanced two explanations for that (1) worldwide scope of the market for loanable funds, (2) the alleged tendency for larger deficits to stimulate the nation's private saving rates: *other things being equal, an increase in the Fed budget deficit should raise interest rates; an increase in borrowing by government implies a right shift in the demand curve for loanable funds* Lloyd (1997).

---

[37] Money view focuses on the liability side of the banks' balance sheet and assumes that changes in monetary aggregates have direct effect on economic activity.

[38] Credit view focuses on the assets side of banks' balance sheet that affect strongly the economic activity more than monetary aggregates.

The previous view was questioned, two explanations support the view that budget deficits do not influence interest rates significantly. Firstly, the financial markets in various nations become integrated, that is worldwide in scope now. This explanation was supported by Lloyd and Abderrezak (1988) that as interest rates, begin to rise in response to heavier government borrowing. However, the quantity of funds available to meet the government demand rises as foreign institutions set up their lending in local funds market. In other words, the supply curve of loanable funds thought to be elastic-almost horizontal - with respect to the interest rate.

The Second explanation, concerns the alleged relationship between government budget deficit and individuals' saving behavior. Suppose the public is looking forward, and recognizes that today's larger budget deficit (BD) implies either higher future taxes or lower future living standard. To protect themselves and their heirs from this expected future belt-tightening, they step up their current saving rates. In this event, loanable funds curve shifts (BL) rightward, tending to neutralize the effect on interest rates. This position is supported by what is known by the Ricardian Equivalent proposition.

In general, banks loans are specified according to the previous factors as following:

$$BL_t = \Theta_0 + \Theta_1 ER_t + \Theta_2 BD_t + \Theta_3 (RM_2B)_t, \quad \Theta_0, \Theta_1, \Theta_2, \Theta_3 >$$

Where $(ER)_t$ is, excess reserves held by the banks, represents their ability to expand credit, on which the central bank has a partial control over via the reserve requirements. $(BD)_t$ is budget deficit reflecting the heavily government borrowing influences to the growth of banks' lending. $(RM2b)_t$ is, real money balances, to capture the public's behavior towards the excessive government borrowing, doing so expecting higher taxes and less standard of living to repay that loans, this consistent with rational behavior of Ricardian equivalence proposition.

24. Velocity of Circulation of Money

Concerning the velocity of circulation of money, the monetarists believe that velocity is stable and predictable (McConnell and Brue, 1993), while from the Keynesian and non-monetarists view it is unstable and unpredictable. For the purpose of conducting monetary policy, economists focus on the volume of expenditures on final goods and services $(GDP)_t$. The implications on monetary policy, as noted by Dornbusch and Fischer (1990, p.377) is that: *With constant velocity of income there is a direct link between nominal income (Y) and the quantity of nominal (M2). Thus, the Fed could determine the path of (Y) by setting the path (M2). But, often (some say always) when stable relationship discovered and started to be used, it breaks down, Good hart's law.* As specified by Lloyd (1997, p.517) the velocity may fluctuate as a result of the following factors; (1) institutional factors such as frequencies and habits of payment, the use of credit cards, and other factors, that govern the degree of synchronization between receipts and payments, and disbursement of funds. (2) Procyclical pattern of interest rates, which represents an opportunity cost of holding money. (3) Financial technology gives the availability of substitutes for money. (4) Economic uncertainty, at any time or event raises the economic agents tendency to hold more money as the safest assts. (5) Expected inflation tempts people to reduce their money holdings in an effort to escape the inflation tax. (6) Income elasticity of money demand, the unity elasticity keep the velocity unchanged, while, greater than one elasticity reduces the velocity, and less than one elasticity increases the velocity. According to the previous specification, the velocity of money will be given in the following functional form:

$$V = \Pi_0 + \Pi_1 P_t + \Pi_2 Dev Y_t + \Pi_3 (M/P)_t + \Pi_4 (QM)_t + \Pi_5 BD$$
$$\Pi_0, \Pi_3, \Pi_4 < 0, \Pi_1, \Pi_2, \Pi_5 > 0$$

where

Π_0	a constant term explains long-term behavior of the velocity circulation of money
P_t	the general price index

QMt	

(Π_0) of equation (11) explains long-term behavior of the velocity which captures the dramatic changes that occurred in financial institutions (Bordo and Jonung, 1990, pp.141-203). The second term, (P_t) is the general price index which represents the opportunity cost of holding money. Velocity response to changes in (P_t) depends on the price level elasticity of demand for money. According to Dornbusch and Fischer (1990, p.379) wrote supporting that: *Inflation implies that money loses purchasing power, and inflation creates a cost of holding money. The higher the rate of inflation, the lower the amount of real balances that will be held. Under conditions of very high-expected inflation, demand for money falls dramatically relative to income velocity rises as people use less money in relation to income.*

The third term of equation (11) reflects the monetarists' point of view that emphasizes the hypothesis that the demand for money is relatively insensitive to interest rates. This is consistent with the prevailing thoughts and religious beliefs in an Islamic country like Sudan, where dealings through interest are forbidden. Lloyd (1997, p.530) accepted the hypothesis developed by Friedman with regard to the procyclical pattern of the velocity that: *"Both consumer expenditures and money demand depend not on current income but on permanent income or long-run average income ..."*

Thus, the second half of a cyclical upswing when

current income or GDP$_t$, (Y$_t$) exceeds permanent income or GDP$_t$, (Y*). However, the demand for money does not keep pace with current GDP$_t$, thus velocity (GDP/M)$_t$ rises. During a recession actual income or GDP (Y) falls below permanent income or GDP (Y*). Again because the demand for money depends on (Y*) its quantity will not decline in proportion to the decline in actual GDP$_t$, velocity (GDP/M)$_t$ falls.

The fourth term reflects the effect of inflation on real money balance (RMB). De Broeck et al (1997, p.31) noted that high and protected inflation during the period preceding the introduction of stabilization program substantially eroded real money balances because, expected developments in inflation, the real exchange rate and the financial system, velocity should follow a downward trend. Because, inflation imposes a tax on the economy, reducing its value at rates equal to the difference between the actual inflation and money rates. Accordingly, Lloyd (1997, p.519) supports the opinion that people reduce their demand for money in an effort to escape the inflation tax: *during hyperinflation, historically, increases in money velocity escalates dramatically as people desperately try to rid themselves of money before its value plunges again.* So the expected sign of real money balance (M/P) in velocity function is supposed to be positive.

The fifth term represents the effect of establishment of an efficient market-based banking and payment systems. De Broeck et al (1997) in the context of explaining and forecasting the velocity of money in eastern Europe and Former Soviet Union concluded that: *the establishment of an efficient market-based banking system, should induce an increase in the degree of monetization of economic transactions and make holding wealth in liquid form more attractive and therefore, be reflected in a downward movement of velocity.* The sign of quasi money $(QM)_t$ in velocity function is expected to be negative. The sixth term captures the effect of the changes in fiscal activities of the government.

Budget Deficit

Concerning budget deficits, McConnell and Brue (1993, p.350-351) wrote that there are three philosophies. The first is an annually balanced budget, which intensifies the economic cycle to maintain a balanced budget. Several prominent economists emphasized this direction. They think that the government has a tendency to grow larger than it should because there is less popular opposition to this growth when it is financed by deficit rather than taxes. However, annually balanced budget philosophy is not economically neutral. The pursuit of such a policy is procyclical, not countercyclical. The second is cyclical balanced budget, for which the government exerts a countercyclical influence and at the same time balances its budget. The weakness of this point of view is that upswings and downswings of the economic cycle may not be of equal magnitude and duration. Hence, the goal of stabilization conflicts with balanced budget over the cycle. Finally, the third philosophy concentrates on the fact that a balanced budget - either annual or cyclical – is secondary. The primary purpose of government finance is to provide for non-inflationary full employment, i.e., to balance the economy, not the budget. If the attainment of this objective means either persistent surplus or a large or growing public debt, so be it:

$$BD_t = \Psi_1 BL_t + \Psi_2 \, DevY_t + \Psi_3 \, INF_t, \quad \Psi_1, \Psi_3 > 0, \, \Psi_2 < 0$$

The first term of Equation (12), captures the third philosophy that budget deficit (BD_t) is just an instrument to achieve and maintain economic stability. According to, Dornbusch and Fischer (1990, p.603): *if there is a primary deficit in the budget, then the total budget deficit will be kept growing as the debt grows because, of the deficit, and the interest payments rise because the debt is growing"*. It follows that total bank loans (BL_t) is expected to have positive impact (Ψ_1) on the budget deficit.

The second term reflects the government systematic response to the economic cycle, $DevY_t$. The actual real GDP deviates from its potential level, both tax receipts and public expenditures respond to that cyclical change. Hence, that produces difference between actual and structural budget deficits, thus, the government has to accommodate its deficit to the level of full employment (Carlson, 1989). In this case, the second philosophy is followed to offset recession, government should lower taxes and increase its expenditures, thereby incurring a deficit, while during the ensuing inflationary upswing, it raises taxes and slashes its expenditures. The resulting surplus could be used to retire government borrowing incurred in financing the recession. In recession where actual Y lags behind Y* we expect a negative Ψ_2 thus, the budget deficit (BD_t) increases.

The third term of equation (12) captures the impact of inflation on budget deficits or the so-called inflation tax. In discussing monetization of deficits, the fact is that financing government spending through the creation of high-powered money is an alternative to explicit taxation. According to Dornbusch and Fischer (1990, p.657):

"when the government finances its deficit by issuing money, which the public adds to its holdings of nominal balances to maintain the real value of money balances constant. We say the government is financing itself through the inflation tax".

The amount of revenue generated is the product of the tax rate (inflation tax, (T_{INF}) and the object of taxation (real monetary base, B) given the real output:

$$T_{INF} = INF_t \times B$$

As Sargent (1982) noted, it was remarkable that hyperinflationary economies incurred large budget deficits and rapid money printing. In several cases, the origin of the budget deficits was wartime spending, which generated large national debts and also destroyed the tax-gathering apparatus of the country Dornbusch and Fischer (1990).

25. Data Assessment and Empirical Results

A system is a group of equations containing unknown parameters. Systems can be estimated using a number of multivariate techniques that take into account the interdependencies among the equations in the system. The most general form of a system is a vector of endogenous variables, a vector of exogenous variables and a vector of possibly serially correlated disturbances. The task of estimation is to find estimates of the vector of parameters. There are a number of methods of estimating the parameters of the system (Amemiya, 1983). A simultaneous estimation approach is to estimate the complete set of parameters of the equations in the system simultaneously. This approach allows for placing constraints on coefficients across equations. In addition, it employs techniques that account for correlation in the residuals across equations. There are important advantages of using a system to estimate parameters. However, these do not come without cost. Most importantly, if one of the equations in the system is mis-specified and its parameters estimated using single equation methods, only the mis-specified equation will be poorly estimated. If a system of estimation techniques is employed, the poor estimates for the misspecification equation may "contaminate" estimates for other equations. Thus, Press et al (1992) distinguished between systems of equations and models. A model is a group of known equations describing endogenous variables. Models are used to solve for values of the endogenous variables, given information on other variables in the model. Systems and models often work together quite closely. The parameters of a system of equations might be estimated, and then a model is created to forecast or simulate values of the endogenous variables in the system. Once the parameters of the system of equations has been estimated, it may be able to forecast future values or perform simulations for different values of the explanatory variables. The model solved can permit forecasting from an estimated system of equations or to perform a single simulation (Quandt, 1983).

To obtain elasticities of the endogenous dependent variables, with respect to their determinant explanatory variables, a log-linear approximation of all system equations previously mentioned were taken around the steady state values of variables, to constitute following system obtained:

$$l_t = \xi_1\, p_t + \xi_2\, bl_t, \qquad\qquad \xi_1 > 0,\ 1 > \xi_2 > 0 \qquad (1$$

$$m_t = m_0 + \alpha y_t + (1-\alpha)l_t + \rho H_t + e_t, \qquad H \geq 0, 0 < \alpha < 1, \rho > 0 \quad (2$$

$$rmb_t = \beta_0 + \beta_1 devy_t + \beta_2 rqm_t + \beta_{31} roex_t^e, \qquad \beta_0\, \beta_1, \beta_2 > 0, \beta_{31} < 0 \quad (3$$

$$dm_t = \gamma_0 + \gamma_1\, (dfm)_t, \qquad\qquad \gamma_0 > 0,\ \gamma_1 > 0 \qquad ($$

$$ad_t = \delta_1 ad_{t-1} + \delta_2 dm_t + \delta_3 v_{2t} + \delta_4 bd_t, \qquad \delta_1, \delta_2, \delta_3, \delta_4 > 0 \qquad (5$$

$$y_t = A + (1-\varepsilon)\, n_t + \varepsilon\, k_t, \qquad\qquad \varepsilon > 0 \qquad (6$$

$$k_t = \varphi_1\, iv_t + \varphi_2\, bd_t, \qquad\qquad \varphi_1 > 0,\ \varphi_2 < 0 \qquad ($$

$$iv_t = \omega_{11} P_t + \omega_{12} S_t + \omega_2\, devy_t, \qquad \omega_{11} > 0, \omega_{12} > 0\ \omega_2 > 0 \qquad ($$

$$inf_t = \lambda_1 ad_{t-1} + \lambda_2 rqm_t + \lambda_3 el_t + \lambda_4 roex_t + e_t \quad \lambda_2, < 0\, \lambda_1, \lambda_3, \lambda_4 > 0$$

$$bl_t = \theta_0 + \theta_1 er_t + \theta_2\, bd_t + \theta_3\, rmb_t \qquad\qquad \theta_0, \theta_1, \theta_2, \theta_3 > 0 \qquad ($$

$$v_{2t} = \pi_0 + \pi_1 pt + \pi_2 devy_t + \pi_3 rm_t + \pi_4 bd_t, \qquad\qquad (1$$

$$\pi_0, \pi_3, < 0,\ \pi_1, \pi_2, \pi_4 > 0$$

$$bd_t = \psi_1 bl_t + \psi_2\, devy_t + \psi_3 inf_t, \qquad\qquad \psi_1, \psi_3 > 0,\ \psi_2 < 0 \qquad ($$

Note: lower case letter indicates the logarithm of a variable (e.g., $m_t = \log M_t$) except the inflation (inf_t) and depreciation (oex_t) rates, where actual figures are used. The notations for interpretation of the variables and parameters symbols are as follows:

The Variables:

el_t — the growth of real effective liquidity.

p_t — the growth of general price level or CPI.

bl_t — the growth of banks' loans.

m_t — the growth of wide money supply.

y_t — the growth of real output.

rmb_t — the growth of real wide money balances or (M2)^d.

$devy_t$ — the growth of deviations of real output from its long-term trend.

qm_t — the growth of financial wealth i.e. quasi money.

oex_t — the rate of depreciation in the value of local currency or official exchange rate.

$(dfm)_t$ — the growth of lags in supply of money process in response to changes in real money balances demand.

dm_t — the growth of adjustment cost.

ad_t — the growth of aggregate demand.

adl_{t-1} the growth of lag aggregate demand.

$v2_t$ the growth of wide money velocity.

bd_t the growth of budget deficit.

n_t the growth of labor force.

k_t the growth of capital stock.

iv_t the growth of private investment.

s_t the growth of private saving.

inf_t the actual rate of inflation.

gdp_t the growth of nominal GDP.

er_t the growth of excess reserves at banks.

The Parameters:

Z_1 the elasticity of effective liquidity demand with respect to (w.r.t.) the growth of price level.

Z_2 the elasticity of effective liquidity demand with respect to the growth of banks' loans.

m_0 the desired money stock as perceived by the Central Bank.

α the elasticity of real money balances w.r.t. real output growth.

$1-\alpha$ the elasticity of real money balances w.r.t. growth of effective liquidity demand, reflect the money supply endogeneity

ρ the elasticity of real money balances w.r.t. the Monetary policy stance.

β_0 desired real money balances.

β_1 the real money balance response to the deviations of real output from its potential long-term level.

β_2 the real money balance response to the development of financial wealth (quasi money).

β_{31} the real money balance response to the depreciation of future purchasing power or depreciation of local currency value

γ_0 a cost parameter adjustment according to the changes in other factors than monetary market impacts.

γ_1 the cost adjustment response as result of monetary market impacts (slowness in adjustment of money stock to the changes in real money balances).

δ_1 the response of aggregate demand to its lagged value, consistent with adaptive expectation concept.

δ_2 the response of aggregate demand to the cost adjustment in domestic monetary sector.

δ_3 the response of aggregate demand to the velocity of money.

δ_4 the response of aggregate demand to the fiscal policy shock.

A   the level of Technical Knowledge.

ε the elasticity of real output w.r.t. the growth in the capital stock.

$1\text{-}\varepsilon$ the elasticity of real output w.r.t. the growth in the labor force size.

φ_1 the response of capital stock to the growth in private investment.

φ_2 the response of capital stock to the growth in budget deficit.

ω_{11} the response of private investment to the growth in the general price level.

ω_{12} the response of private investment to the growth in the private saving.

ω_2 the response of private investment to the growth in deviations of real output to its potential long-term trend.

λ_1 the long-term response of inflation rate to changes in past growth in aggregate demand, consistent with the adaptive expectations.

λ_2 the response of inflation rate to the changes in real growth of quasi money.

λ_3 the response of inflation rate to the growth in effective liquidity demand.

λ_4 the response of inflation rate to the real growth of depreciation in domestic currency value (S.D. value of U.S. Dollars)

θ_0 desired level of banks loans.

θ_1 the response of banks' loans to the growth in excess reserves of the banks.

θ_2 the response of banks loans to the growth in budget deficit.

θ_3 the response of banks loans to the growth in real money balances.

π_0 the short-term velocity level, regarded as constant.

π_1 the response of money velocity to the growth in the general price level.

π_2 the response of money velocity to the growth in deviations of real output from its potential long-term trend.

π_3 the response of money velocity to the growth in real money balances.

π_4 the response of money velocity to the growth in financial wealth (quasi money).

π_5 the response of money velocity to the growth in budget deficit.

ψ_1 the response of budget deficit to the growth in banks' loans.

ψ_2 the response of budget deficit to the growth in the deviations of real output from its long-term trend.

ψ_3 the response of budget deficit to the growth in to inflation rate.

z a portion of bank loans (Bl_t) that individuals prefer to hold as liquid money holdings.

J constant ratio of change in desired capital stock to changes in output.

Data Assessment[39]

Effective liquidity, el_t, is a proxy for money demand by the public as perceived by the BOS. Measured here by

---

[39] For prior diagnosing the growth relationships between used explanatory variables and its dependent ones, see the appendix 3, figure 3, diagrams 5-13.

M1, obtained by the sum of cash money held by the public and demand deposits or $M_1 = C_P + DD$. The General Price Index, P_t, is measured as an average price of higher, medium, and lower income groups, base year (1990=100), and its source is the Central Bureau of Statistics: Sudan. The total bank loans are annual calculations of the BOS, measured in millions of Sudanese pounds.

The supply of money, M_t, is measured as broad money concept M_2, i.e., (M_1+quasi money), reflects the BOS perceptions when initiating money.

The Gross Domestic Product, GDP, is measured in LS millions of Sudanese Pounds at current prices for the period 1979/80-1998 and a preliminary estimates for 1969-2002 (Central Bureau of Statistics: Sudan). Then, GDP is deflated by the general price index to obtain the real output, Y.

For the economic cycle influence variables in the system, a proxy is constructed to capture its effects. Thus, the economic cycle is approximated by, $DevY_t$, the deviations of real output, Y, from its potential levels or its long-term trend (Y^*). The latter is estimated as a time series trend function of Eviews - an econometrics computer program- normalizing the data to (0) in the observations period starting from the first observation.

The demand for money is the demand for real money

balances (M_t/P_t), where $M_t = M_2$, is measuring its growth by subtracting the growth of general price index from nominal money growth. M_2 data found in annual basis in BOS Annual Reports.

Concerning the actual rate of inflation, INF_t, it is measured by the percentage changes in the annual general price index as reported by the BOS. The anticipation of inflation rate is assumed to be adaptive expectations i.e., $NF_t^e = INF_{t-1}$. The depreciation rate of local currency, OEX, also reflects the effect of depreciation of future purchasing power on real money balances. Proxied by the official exchange value of US dollar in Sudanese Pounds. The OEX is measured as predetermined by the BOS and as declared by the free foreign exchange market. The source is the Research Department, the BOS.

Quasi money, QM_t, is employed as a proxy for the impact of financial wealth (W). It is measured in LS million. The source comes from the Annual reports, the BOS.

The cost of resources adjustment, dM_t, represents the discrepancies between the money holdings and the money supply. It reflects real resources spent for the reallocation to match the money holdings with the stock available (Choi and Seonghwan Oh, 2000, p.8). It is measured as the difference between actual money stock (M_2) and actual real balances, M/P. while dFM_t, is the result of money market interactions which represents the lag in accommodation of money supply to the changes in the demand for real money balances. The latter is measured as the difference between estimated values of real money balances and money supply.

Aggregate demand, AD_t, is represented by total nominal income at current prices for the period 1969/70-1997, measured in LS million as reported by the Central Bureau of Statistics.

Broad money velocity, V_{2t}, is calculated as a proportion of GDP to M_2. Budget deficit, BD, is measured at its current level as reported in Annual Reports of the BOS.

The national labor force, N_t, are approximated as 30% of annual size of Sudan population (in Million) through out the study period.

The national capital, K_t, is estimated as follows: $K_t = (1-d)K_{t-1} + I_t$, where $K_{t-1} = K_0 + I_{t-1}$ and d is an annual rate of capital depreciation, assumed to be 0.0212 following Dotsey (1984, p.3-12) and Choi and Ho (1999). The previous year capital stock, K_{t-1}, depend on an initial capital stock, K_0, and the previous private investment. The K_0, equals to the current private savings for the year 1971 (LS 110.4 million). Both private savings, S_t, and investment, I_t, are measured at current prices for 1969/70-1997.

Excess reserve of banks, ER_t, is calculated as total banks' deposits excluding investment deposits minus the amount of reserve requirements

The Econometric Method

Weighted Two-Stage Least Squares. The System Estimation Method is weighted two-stage least squares (WTSLS). As noted by Pindyck and Rubinfeld (1998) the WTSLS is an appropriate technique when some of the right-hand side variables are correlated with the error terms, and there is heteroskedasticity, but no contemporaneous correlation in the residuals. The main steps, is to apply TSLS to the un-weighted system so as to enforce any cross-equation parameter restrictions. Then, the results from this estimation are used to form equation weights, based upon the estimated equation variances. If there are no cross-equation restrictions, these first-stage results will be identical to un-weighted single-equation TSLS (Davidson and MacKinnon, 1993, pp.221-224) and (Johnston and DiNardo, 1997).

26.   Indicators of the Summary Statistics

The t-statistic, which is computed as the ratio of an estimated coefficient to its standard error, is used to test the hypothesis that a coefficient is equal to zero. To get an interpretation of the t-statistic, the probability distribution of the t must be observed. The probability of calculated t-statistic gives the coefficient an average value equal to zero. Hence the Probability distribution of t of the estimated results coefficients shows the probability of drawing a t-statistic as extreme as the one actually observed. That is true under the assumption that the errors are normally distributed. Moreover, the estimated coefficients are asymptotically normally distributed. This probability is also known as the p-value or the marginal significance level. Given a p-value, you can tell at a glance if you reject or accept the hypothesis that the true coefficient is zero against a two-sided alternative that it differs from zero. For example, if the test at the 5% significance level performed, a p-value lower than .05 is taken as evidence to reject the null hypothesis of a zero coefficient.

The error tem reports the estimated standard errors of the estimated coefficients. The standard errors measure the statistical reliability of the coefficient estimates-the larger the standard errors, the more statistical noise in the estimates. If the errors are normally distributed, there are about 2 chances in 3 that the true regression coefficient lies within one standard error of the reported coefficient, and 95 chances out of 100 that it lies within two standard errors.

The R-squared (R^2) statistic measures the success of the regression in predicting the values of the dependent variable within the sample. Moreover, it can be defined as the fraction of the variance of the dependent variable explained by the independent variables. The R^2 statistic will equal one if the regression fits perfectly and zero if it fits no better than the simple mean of the dependent variable. It can be negative if the regression does not have an intercept or constant, or if the estimation method is two-stage least squares.

EViews computes the (centered) as:

$$R^2 = 1 - \frac{\hat{e}'\hat{e}}{(y - \bar{y})'(y - \bar{y})}$$

$$\hat{e} = y - Xb,$$

$$\bar{y} = \frac{\sum\limits_{i=1}^{T} y_i}{T}$$

Where

$\hat{e}$ Is the T-vector of estimate residual

Y Is a T-dimensional vector containing observations on the dependant variable

$\bar{y}$ Is the mean of the dependent (left hand) variable.

$\hat{e}'$ Is an inverse vector of T- vector estimated residuals

$\hat{e}'\hat{e}$ Equal $\sum\limits_{i=1}^{T}(y_i - Xb)^2$

T Is the number of observations

B Is regression K-vector of estimated coefficients, calculated as $b = (X'X)^{-1}X'Y$

X   Is a T×K matrix of independent variables

X'   Is an inverse of the T×K matrix of independent variables

Adjusted R-squared $\overline{R}^2$

One problem with using of R^2 as a measure of goodness of fit is that it will never decrease as you add more regressors. In the extreme case, you can always obtain an increased value of one if you include as many independent regressors as there are sample observations.

Therefore, the adjusted R^2, commonly denoted as $\overline{R}^2$, penalizes for the addition of regressors, which do not contribute to the explanatory power of the model. The adjusted R^{-2} is computed as:

$$\overline{R}^2 = 1 - (1 - R^2)\frac{T-1}{T-K}$$

The $\overline{R}^2$ is never larger than the R^2. Moreover, the $\overline{R}^2$ decreases as long as you add regressors, and for poorly fitting models, may becomes negative.

The Durbin-Watson statistic

The Durbin-Watson statistic is a test for first-order serial correlation. More formally, the DW statistic measures the linear association between adjacent residuals from a regression model. As noted by Johnston and DiNardo (1997), the Durbin-Watson is a test of the hypothesis =0 in the specification:

$$DW = \frac{\sum\limits_{i=2}^{T} (\hat{e}_i - \hat{e}_{i-1})}{\sum\limits_{i=1}^{T} \hat{e}_i}$$

If there is no serial correlation, the DW statistic will be around 2. The DW statistic will fall below 2 if there is positive serial correlation -in the worst case, it will be near zero. If there is negative correlation, the statistic will lie somewhere between 2 and 4.

Positive serial correlation is the most commonly observed form of dependence. Nsur (1997, p.223, et seq.) argued that what is known is that DW statistic distributed between some upper and lower values of tabulated DW statistic. As a rule of thumb, with 50 or more observations and only a few independent variables, a DW statistic below about 1.5 is a strong indication of positive first order serial correlation. However, it becomes a serious problem as the value of calculated DW is very close to 1 or near to 4.

Johnston and DiNardo (1997) made a discussion on the Durbin-Watson test and the table of the significance points of the statistic. They noted that there are three main limitations of the DW test as a test for serial correlation. First, the distribution of the DW statistic under the null hypothesis depends on the data matrix, x. The usual approach to handling this problem is to place bounds on the critical region, creating a region where the test results are inconclusive. Second, if there are lagged dependent variables on the right-hand side of the regression, the DW test is no longer valid[40]. Finally, you may only test the null hypothesis of no serial correlation against the alternative hypothesis of first-order serial correlation.

27. The Empirical Results

The equations system is estimated by using Iterative Weighted Two-Stage Least Squares (IWTSLS), employing time series data for the Sudan Economy covering the period (1972-2001), included 30 observations, total system (unbalanced) observations, and achieving convergence after: 1 weight matrix, 2 total coefficients iterations; the results were obtained as follows:

Table (4-10)

The Model Estimation Results

---

[40] There are better tests for serial correlation testing than the DW statistic, such as the Q-statistic and the Breusch-Godfrey LM test. Both of them are more general tests of serial correlation than the Durbin-Watson test (Dezhbaksh, 1990, 126–132).

Prob.	t-Statistic	Std. Error	Coefficient	
0.0347	2.120774	0.039529	0.083832	$C(1) = \zeta_1$
0.0000	43.44629	0.024458	1.062606	$C(2) = \zeta_2$
0.0545	1.929917	0.030832	0.059503	$C(3) = m_0$
0.5177	0.647653	0.002265	0.001467	$C(4) = \alpha$
0.0000	440.8609	0.002265	0.998533	$C(5) = \alpha - 1$
0.0000	23.42211	0.039161	0.917243	$C(6) = \beta_1$
0.0000	-6.146017	4.29E-05	-0.000264	$C(7) = \beta_2$
0.0000	15.94496	0.000178	0.002836	$C(8) = \beta_3$
0.0000	14.46400	0.443140	6.409585	$C(9) = \gamma_0$
0.0000	10.95953	0.290538	3.184165	$C(10) = \gamma_1$
0.0000	10.87408	0.086406	0.939587	$C(11) = \delta_1$
0.0818	-1.745812	0.095059	-0.165955	$C(12) = \delta_2$
0.0195	2.348045	0.245825	0.577209	$C(13) = \delta_3$
0.0163	2.414820	0.163142	0.393959	$C(14) = \delta_4$
0.0001	-3.984040	8.361052	-33.31077	$C(15) = A$
0.0000	4.225083	1.019981	4.309503	$C(16) = 1 - \varepsilon$
0.0000	10.72001	0.069433	0.744319	$C(17) = \varepsilon$
0.0000	13.72020	0.069437	0.952683	$C(18) = \varphi_1$
0.8340	0.209753	0.117261	0.024596	$C(19) = \varphi_2$
0.0000	17.35603	0.053705	0.932099	$C(20) = \omega_{11}$
0.0570	1.910489	0.032470	0.062033	$C(21) = \omega_{12}$
0.0000	30.48160	0.023356	0.711919	$C(22) = \omega_2$
0.0022	3.082451	0.075999	0.234264	$C(23) = \nu_1$
0.0000	-37139.33	2.69E-05	-1.000074	$C(24) = \nu_2$
0.0000	5.466248	0.131308	0.717765	$C(25) = \nu_3$
0.0000	8.603472	0.090178	0.775846	$C(26) = \nu_4$
0.0264	2.231081	0.053259	0.118826	$C(27) = \theta_1$
0.2473	1.159071	0.056077	0.064997	$C(28) = \theta_2$
0.0000	10.78183	0.069561	0.749995	$C(29) = \theta_3$
0.0000	164.6479	0.006005	0.988629	$C(30) = \pi_1$
0.0000	229.4320	0.004362	1.000717	$C(31) = \pi_2$
0.0000	-174.8654	0.005645	-0.987050	$C(32) = \pi_3$
0.0000	22.31874	0.042575	0.950212	$C(33) = \psi_1$

0.0000	-9.183183	0.052466	-0.481803	$C(34) = \psi_2$
0.0264	2.229765	0.003416	0.007616	$C(35) = \psi_3$
Observations: 30		5.50E-16	Determinant residual covariance	

Equation: Equation: $eL_t = \zeta_1 P_t + \zeta_2 BL_t$ _____ (1)

9.577855	Mean dependent var	0.986517	R-squared
3.524543	S.D. dependent var	0.986036	Adjusted R-squared
4.857104	Sum squared resid	0.416495	S.E. of regression
		2.094335	Durbin-Watson stat

Equation: $M_t = m_0 Pt + \alpha\, TRY + (1- \alpha)eL_t$ _____ (2)

9.957805	Mean dependent var	0.981402	R-squared
3.755219	S.D. dependent var	0.980024	Adjusted R-squared
7.605689	Sum squared resid	0.530747	S.E. of regression
		1.730576	Durbin-Watson stat

Equation: $RM1B = \beta_1 DEVY_t + \beta_2 RQM_t + \beta_3 ROEX_t$ _____ (3)

8.929515	Mean dependent var	0.897675	R-squared
2.766829	S.D. dependent var	0.890096	Adjusted R-squared
22.71656	Sum squared resid	0.917253	S.E. of regression
		1.758255	Durbin-Watson stat

Equation: $DM1_t = \gamma_0 + \gamma_1 DFM_t$ _____ (4)

9.700704	Mean dependent var	0.800148	R-squared
4.060881	S.D. dependent var	0.793011	Adjusted R-squared
95.57541	Sum squared resid	1.847541	S.E. of

			regression
		0.848676	Durbin-Watson stat

Equation: $AD_t = \delta_1 LAGAD_t + \delta_2 RDMl_t + \delta_3 V_t + \delta_4 BD_t$ ___(5)

11.86997	Mean dependent var	0.963050	R-squared
4.542120	S.D. dependent var	0.958786	Adjusted R-squared
22.10723	Sum squared resid	0.922105	S.E. of regression
		1.840034	Durbin-Watson stat

Equation: $GDPT = A + (1 - \varepsilon)\, N_t + \varepsilon\, K_t$ ___(6)

11.47013	Mean dependent var	0.983470	R-squared
3.563218	S.D. dependent var	0.982246	Adjusted R-squared
6.086248	Sum squared resid	0.474781	S.E. of regression
		2.025780	Durbin-Watson stat

Equation: $K_t = \varphi_1 IV_t + \varphi_2 BD_t$ ___(7)

9.290812	Mean dependent variable	0.944386	R-squared
3.449663	S.D. dependent var	0.942399	Adjusted R-squared
19.19280	Sum squared resid	0.827923	S.E. of regression
		2.523602	Durbin-Watson stat

Equation: $IV_t = \omega_{11} P_t + \omega_{12} S_t + \omega_2 DEVY_t$ ___(8)

9.538409	Mean dependent var	0.977755	R-squared
3.661674	S.D. dependent var	0.976107	Adjusted R-squared
8.649600	Sum squared resid	0.566000	S.E. of regression
		2.000023	Durbin-Watson stat

Equation: $INF_t = v_1LAGAD_t + v_2RQM_t + v_3EL_t + v_4ROEX_t$ _____ (9)

44.25800	Mean dependent var	1.000000	R-squared
38.10911	S.D. dependent var	1.000000	Adjusted R-squared
0.000984	Sum squared resid	0.006152	S.E. of regression
		2.460134	Durbin-Watson stat

Equation: $BL_t = \theta_1ER_t + \theta_2BD_t + \theta_3EL_t$ _____ (10)

8.655911	Mean dependent var	0.985510	R-squared
3.031269	S.D. dependent var	0.984437	Adjusted R-squared
3.861015	Sum squared resid	0.378154	S.E. of regression
		1.814778	Durbin-Watson stat

Equation: $V_t = \pi_1P_t + \pi_2DEVY_t + \pi_3RM_t$ _____ (11)

1.512323	Mean dependent var	0.999158	R-squared
0.643426	S.D. dependent var	0.999096	Adjusted R-squared
0.010108	Sum squared resid	0.019349	S.E. of regression
		1.369983	Durbin-Watson stat

Equation: $BD_t = \psi_1BL_t + \psi_2DEVY_t + \psi_3INF_t$ _____ (12)

5.227179	Mean dependent var	0.953517	R-squared
3.072105	S.D. dependent var	0.950073	Adjusted R-squared
12.72235	Sum squared resid	0.686439	S.E. of regression
		2.212430	Durbin-Watson stat

28.   Statistical Analysis

Estimation result of equation (1) in Table (4-10) showed that both the general price index and banks loans growth rates are significant in affecting the growth of effective liquidity. In general, the above two regressors explained 98.6% of the variability in the effective liquidity demand. Meanwhile, the reported value of DW statistic (2.09) is biased to the value 2 for the equation (1) used no intercept.

Concerning estimation result of equation (2) in Table (4-10), money supply growth was significant and directly affected by the price index. Meanwhile, the trend of real output showed insignificant direct effect on money supply growth. According to p-value it is reasonably to reject the effect of output trend on money supply growth. The effective liquidity has scored the most significant direct effect (440.861) on the money supply growth. The three variables explained 97.8% of variations in the money supply. The reported D-W (2.41) is lie within accepted region indicating no serial correlation.

With regard to the estimated equation (3), revealed that real money balances are affected directly significant by cyclical fluctuations of real output around its potential trend and adversely significant by the growth in the real value of quasi money. While, the depreciation in the real value of Sudanese Pound emerges less negative significance. The overall significance of previous regressors explained 63% of the variations in the real money balances. The reported D-W that no serial correlation.

The result of equation (4) statistically, indicated that the cost of resources adjustment could be explained very significant through the positive growth in the difference between money balances and money supply. The included regressors here explained 97.5% of the variations in the growth of the cost resources adjustment.

The result of equation (5) indicated that the growth in aggregate demand in Sudan is significant directly, affected directly significant by its lagged values and adversely less significant by the velocity of circulating money. Moreover, it affected significantly positive by the budget deficits and the cost of resources adjustment. However, the lagged aggregate demand values have scored the higher significance in affecting its current values. Those explanatory variables explained 97% of the variations in aggregate demand growth. With regard to the real output growth in equation (6), it is clear that Both the capital growth and the constant term which measures the level of technical knowledge have provided a very significant positive effect on the real output growth. Adversely, the labor force growth in Sudan showed a insignificant and negative impact on the real output growth. The overall significance of the two explanatory variables explained 97% of the variations in the real output growth.

The empirical result in equation (7) stated that the capital growth in Sudan is affected directly and significantly by the growth in the private investment, while the government incurring of budget deficits has positive but insignificant effect on the capital growth. Both previous two variables explained 95% of the variations in capital growth.

For the private investment growth, the estimated result of equation (8) emphasized that both the real output fluctuations around its potential trend and the general price index have direct and very high significant effect on private investment growth. In contrast, private saving growth was less significant. The overall influence of the three explanatory variables are explaining 98% of the variations in the function of investment growth. The reported D-W (2.00) indicates that no serial correlation, because its value lied just on the mean value of hypothetical D-W value within the acceptance region the null hypothesis. According to the demand pull inflation point of view, equation (9) emerged that actual inflation rate is adversely very significant affected by the growth in real value of quasi money. In the meantime, the depreciation in local currency real value, effective liquidity and one-year lag of aggregate demand have positive and significant effects on inflation rates. The four explanatory variables are fully, explained the variations in actual rate of inflation. With regard to bank loans, the result in equation (10) suggested that bank loans is determined directly more significant by effective liquidity growth rate and significantly direct by the bank excess reserves. Whereas, the growth in budget deficits showed less direct effect on the bank loans growth. The overall influence of the included three explanatory variables is explained about 98% of the variations in the banks loans growth. For the money velocity in Sudan, the result equation (11) showed that there was a very significant positive effect from the real output deviations from its potential trend. Moreover, money velocity directly significant affect by the growth in general price index. Meanwhile, it showed high negative significance to the growth in money supply. The overall influence of those explanatory variables explained about 99.9% of the variations in money velocity.

Finally, the estimated result of equation (12) indicated that current budget deficit growth is statistically very significant affected by growth in bank loans and affected significantly direct by the inflation rate. However, there significant negative effect from the real output deviations to the budget deficit growth. The overall influence of the included three explanatory variables explained about 95% of the variations in the function of budget deficit growth. The reported D-W (2.21) indicates that its value lies within the acceptance region that the null hypothesis i.e., no serial correlation.

29.   Economic Interpretations

Proxied by the effective liquidity demand, economic monetization in Sudan depends mainly on the process of supplying bank loans. The bank loans in turn, is determined through behavior of the banks, the Government incurring of budget deficit, and the public behavior of maintaining their liquidity. Moreover, the results indicated that the banks' ability to form excess reserves has played a major role in facilitating the process of supplying banks loans (equation land 10).

Furthermore, the public's demand for effective liquidity has the most respectable influence on the growth of bank loans for the same period. Accordingly, it could be said that there is an interdependence between the public's demand for effective liquidity and bank loans growth. With regard to the money supply in Sudan, the results proved that it is endogenously determined. Both the perceived general price index and the real output trend have played small role in money supply process. Meanwhile, the growth in the demand for effective liquidity provided the most significant variations in the monetary process. This result support the fact that the BOS attempt to control money supply as an exogenous policy target will be very difficult.

The Impact of the Growth in Bank loans on macroeconomic variables (inf_t, ad_t, gdp_t, v_t, bd_t, Iv_t, k_t) could be determined through two main channels; (1) the effective liquidity demand channel, (2) the budget deficit channel.

The first channel emphasizes that the growth in bank loans could strongly influence effective liquidity demand (equation 1). Which in turn rapidly, may affect the rate of inflation (equation 9) and/or may affect the growth in effective liquidity again. The BOS can induce the monetary process only through the perception of the later and the former (equation 2). The Result revealed that Monetization in Sudan for the study period depend directly on the availability of Banks loans. And Money Supply is respectably endogenous macroeconomic variable mainly determined by liquidity preference of the public, but less significant affected by the price level, and insignificant by the trend of real output. However, money supply in Sudan showed respectable endogeneity. With regard to the impact of bank loans expansion on Sudan economy. it may raise liquidity preference or directly may aggravate inflation. Also, it may induce a monetary growth by the BOS, raising cost of resources adjustment and aggregate demand which feeds the inflation. But inflation growth may exceeds the monetary growth. So, real money growth falls and slowdown money velocity. In that event, it may cause economic recession. On the other hand, the expansion of bank loans may encourage the government to incur large deficits, thus pulling the aggregate demand. Then inflation may be raised with no effect on the real side of the economy.

Finally, the research recommended that to control monetization process, the monetary authorities must control banks' ability to expand loans, good perception to the growth in liquidity preference, and minimizing of the government borrowing. To control liquidity preference the government borrowing must be directed and the policy must be of minimum impact on inflation. To avoid high liquidity preference associated with less velocity, the policy must be designed to facilitate bank loans and to direct it to prior productive sectors. Moreover, the government borrowing must be rationed.

The generated monetary process could affect the aggregate demand (equation 5) via two routes. The first route is that it may change the adjustment cost of resources (equation 4). However, That might be a weak route to motivate growth in the aggregate demand (equation 5). The second route, is that monetary growth may strongly decelerate the velocity of circulating money (equation 11). Hence, this decelerated money velocity may strongly contribute in slowness of the aggregate demand growth. Furthermore, induces the recessional features as it was happened in the Sudan economy during the 1990s decade (equation 5).

The second channel of bank loans to influence the aggregate demand and supply in Sudan is via Government budget deficits. Bank loans is the major factor that may affect the growth of budget deficit (equation 12). In turn, the growth in the budget deficit may considerably affect the aggregate demand (equation 5). Moreover, the budget deficit also might affect the level of GDP growth through the process of capital accumulation. The Capital stock is largely contributing to accelerate the growth of the GDP. However, the most source of growth in the capital is private investment (equation 8) not the budget deficit. This may bring an evidence that most money-financing to the budget in Sudan was to facilitate the current public expenditures rather than developmental expenditures. Accordingly, the incurred budget deficits failed to enhance the capital accumulation and economic growth in Sudan during that period (equation5).

The result also, showed that private investment is determined mainly by the general price index and the deviations of real output from its potential long-term trend. Meanwhile, the private savings contribution was inconsiderable. This could be interpreted as follows, since the Sudan is one of LDCs, the private savings is expected to be small as a result of low level of incomes. The demand for real money balances (equation 3) is affected more rapidly by the deviations of real output from its potential long-term trend. Moreover, it is also affected adversely by the real value of financial instruments. This result supports the fact that people in Sudan build their money balances according to their increasing needs to maintain its real value from deteriorating as result of prices increases, in addition, for transactions in goods and services. While, they intend to reduce their money balances as far as financial services are developed. Furthermore, the demand for real money balances is affected largely by adverse effect of the depreciation in real value of local currency. This factor could be interpreted as an opportunity cost of holding money balances. On the other hand, the impact of money balances growth lied directly on the adjustment cost of resources i.e., the discrepancies between the growth of real money balances and the money supply growth. When money supply lag behind the demand for real money balances. In that case, a positive influence will be on the cost of adjusting balances from other assets to liquid money balances (equation 4). As it were mentioned previously, the growth in the cost adjustment might generate the growth of aggregate demand (equation 5). In turn would shoot the rate of inflation upward through its lagged values (equation 9).

30.   Conclusions

The research attempted to specify the main determinants of cash outflow from banking sector and to capture its major impact on Sudan economy during 1972-2001. A model of twelve equations were formed introducing as endogenous variables: the effective money demand, money supply, real balances, cost of resources adjustment, aggregate demand, the GDP, the capital, private investment, inflation rate, bank loans, velocity of circulating money, and the budget deficit. Where the exogenous variables were: general price index, the real output deviations, quasi money, real local currency exchange rate, the labor force, private savings and bank excess reserves. To obtain the results, the research apply the econometric method IW2SLS.

We summarize and put the next points as follows:

1. Monetization in Sudan for the study period depends directly on the availability of Banks loans.
2. Money Supply is greatly an endogenous macroeconomic variable mainly determined by liquidity preference of the public, but less significant affect by the price level, and insignificant by the trend of real output.
3. The expansion in bank loans causes the following impacts, enhance inflationary pressures via increasing liquidity demand, enhance monetary growth via perception of CBS to the growth in the demand for liquidity, which in turn rises resources cost of adjustment, pulling up the aggregate demand and thus inflationary pressures.
4. Monetary growth which may be associated with slow down of money velocity, so the economy may suffer some recessional features and encourage large deficits by the Government, which may pull aggregate demand causing the inflationary pressures.
5. Expansions in bank loans causes no effect on the real side of the economy.

The Policy Implications: (Monetary growth shock)

1- The impacts of raising reserve requirements:

1. Creating an inflationary process which may cause declining real monetary growth and may de-

accelerate money velocity causing pulling downs in aggregate demand.
2. Resulting in high cost of resources adjustment.
3. Excessive reserves at banks may be declined absorbing the banks' ability of expanding loans. This may reflect as fall in monetary growth, deflationary process and recession.
4. The shock may leave the real side (GDP) with very less effects.

2- Easing Reserves Requirements

1. Directly increase Banks' ability of expanding loans, which may cause inflationary pressures via growth of liquidity preference associated with less monetary growth.
2. additional supply of bank loans may encourage the Government to incur large deficits and may be on account of the private part of aggregate demand.
3. This shock may fail to bring real economic growth.
4. Planned Budget deficit can result in raising percentage of the government borrowing from the Banking system may reduce the current budget deficit and produce less inflationary process.

Thus, monetization must be controlled via control of:

1. Banks' ability to expand loans.
2. Good perception by the BOS to changes occurs in Liquidity preference.
3. Sizing of Government borrowing.

Control of liquidity preference may be via:

1. Control of Government fiscal decision concerning its borrowing from Banks to cover its deficits.
2. Avoidance of inflationary monetary policies.

3. Wise Policies to facilitate finance to the private productive sector.
4. To avoid high liquidity preference and less monetary growth associated downward trend of money velocity Government borrowing must be rationed and Bank loans must be channeled to the productive real sectors.
5. Developing real sources to finance the current budget deficit such as direct taxes, profits of public productive institutions and projects.

(1) The process of monetization in Sudan depends directly on the available bank loans. The latter is determined by the volume of excess reserves held by banks, the Government budget deficits, and the demand for effective money liquidity by the public respectively.

(2) Money supply in Sudan is greatly an endogenous variable determined mainly by the demand for effective money liquidity by the public, with less significance by the general price level index. But its responsiveness to the growth in the trend of real output was insignificant.

(3) The impact of loan expansion by the banking system on the macroeconomic level could be channeled through two main routes; the first, either directly by increasing the effective demand for liquid money. However, that may aggravate the inflationary process in the economy. Indirectly, that an increase in liquid money demand may be percept by the BOS. Accordingly, it may induce a monetary supply growth. That in turn, may raise the cost of resources adjustment. The overall of that process may end by pulling up the aggregate demand thus aggravate inflation in the economy. On the other hand, if the monetary growth associated with an inflationary process it may reduce the money supply in real terms and de-

accelerate its velocity. Hence more, expectations of slowdowns in aggregate demand merges and a deflationary process began. That process may end with recessional features in the economy. The second, Bank loans expansion also may encourage the Government to incur large deficits. That events also may strongly pull the aggregate demand. However, this financial expansion seems to commit less impact on the economic development (the GDP growth). The reason is that most of the banks loans devoted to finance the budget deficit were directed to the current expenditures.

31. Recommendations

(1) Monetization in Sudan could be monitored through: control of banks ability to expand loans, good perception of the BOS to the growth in liquidity preference and the government good control and sizing of its borrowings to cover its budget deficits.

(2) There are some factors play a serious role in growth of liquidity preferences: the government decision of reducing its deficits through borrowing from banking system, the inflationary process rising from expansionary monetary policy and the disturbing of monetary growth. It is that rises the cost of resource adjustment in the economy and aggravates inflation. To avoid high liquidity preference policy must be designed to bring as possible, minimum inflationary process.

(3) Financial expansion through bank loans often activates liquidity preference, encourage the government deficits, and feeds the inflationary process at last. It causes no effects on the real side of the economy. The policy here is to facilitate direct finance to enhance the private investment which could play a vital role in

accumulating capital then enhancement of economic development.

(4) Strong expansion of bank loans if associated with de-accelerated velocity i.e., a large liquidity preference, could produce lower monetary growth and a deflationary process. Moreover, the economy may suffer deep recession. The policy here is to monitor and rationed the government borrowing. Hence, the available bank loans is to be directed to the real productive sectors according to its priorities. That is to avoid declining of money velocity and recessional features in the economy.

32.   References

1. Ahmed, Mohammed Osman, Imad Mohammed, and Selah Eden El-Mahi (1998), "The Causes of Cash outflow form the Banking System in Sudan," An article by, El Masrafi Journal, Vol. 16, Bank of Sudan, Research Department (in Arabic).
2. Ahmed, Sedahmed Mohammed (2000): "Evaluating Cash liquidity and Profitability of Sudanese Commercial Banks", a complementary dissertation submitted in partial fulfillment for M. Sc. Degree in Business Administration, Sudan University, (in Arabic).
3. Amemiya, Takeshi (1983) "Nonlinear Regression Models," Chapter 6 in Handbook of Econometrics, Volume 1, North-Holland.
4. Anthony, S. Campagna (1974), Macroeconomics Theory and Policy, Houghton Miffin Co., USA.
5. Assayed, Osman Ibrahim (1998), The Sudan Economy, 2nd edition, Ommdurman University Press, Sudan.

6. Awad, M. H. (1995): An essay in Al-Masrafi, Quarterly Magazine, Vol. March 1995, Bank of Sudan.

7. Barrel, R. (2002), "The UK and EMU: Choosing the Regime," National Institute of Economic Review No. 180, April.

8. Barrel, R. and Karen Durry (2000), "Choosing the Regime: Macroeconomic Effects of UK entry into EMU" Journal of Common Market Studies, Vol. 30 (4).

9. Barrel, R., D. Karen, and I. Hurst (1999), "An encompassing Framework for Evaluating Simple Monetary Policy Rules," Working Papers, NIESR, London, U.K.K. Durry@niesr.ac.uk

10. Barrel, R., Dawn Holland and Kateøina Šmídková (2003), "An Empirical Analysis of Monetary Policy Choices in Pr-EMU Period," National Institute of Economic and Social Research, Czech and U.K. National Banks. dhollan@niesr.ac.uk, rbarrell@niesr.ac.uk, Katrina.Smidkova@cnb.cz .

11. Baskin, M. (1988), "Symposium on the Slowdown in Productivity Growth," Journal of Economic Perspectives, the chairman of the council of economic advisor. Cit. Dornbusch and Fischer (1990).

12. Batten, Dallas S., Michael P. Blackwell, In-Su Kim, Simon E. Nocera, and Yuzuru Ozeki (1990), "The Conduct of Monetary Policy in the Major Industrial Countries: Instruments and Operating Procedures," Occasional Paper 70, International Monetary Fund.

13. Bernanke, B. (1983), "The Determinants of Investment: Another Look," American Economic Review, Papers and Proceedings, May.

14. Blanchette, Jude (Winter 2005), "Anderson, Hazlitt, and The Quantity Theory of Money", Journal of Libertarian Studies, Vol. 19, No.1.

15. Bouzou, Nicolas (no date), "How Should We Define the Money Supply ? Austrian Versus Monetarist Approach," Seminar Jean-Baptists Say, University Paris-Dauphine, France. Nicolasbouzou@excite.com .

16. Branson, William H. (1977), "Assets Markets and Relative Prices in Exchange Rate Determination," in Sozial wissenschaftliche Annalen des Instituts für Höhere Studien, Reihe A, 1.

17. Brunner, K. and A. H. Meltzer (1990), "Money Supply: A handbook of Monetary Economics," Volume 1, Editors: B. M. Friedman and F. H. Hahn, Amsterdam: North-Holland.

18. Carlson, Keith (1989), "Federal Budget Trendsand the 1981 Reagan Economic Plan", Federal Reserve Bank of St. Louis Review, January/ February.

19. Centre of Strategic Studies, Sudan Strategic Report, 1997, Published on May 1998.

20. Choi, Woon Gyu and Seonghwan Oh (1999), "A Money Demand Function with output Uncertainty, Monetary Uncertainty, and Financial Annovations," Working Paper, Hong Kong University of Science and Technology (August).

21. Choi, Woon Gyu and Seonghwan Oh (2000), "Endogenous Money Supply and Money Demand," IMF Working Papers, 188.

22. Chung, Kyu-Yung (Sebt.17, 2000), "The Role of Central Banks in Currency Crises: With Special Reference to Korea's experience in recovering from the currency crisis", A conference of Challenges to

Central Banking from Globlized Financial System, at the IMF, Washington, D.C.

23. Clarida, Richard, Jordi Gali and Mark Gertler (1998), Monetary Policy Rules in Practice: Some International Evidence, European Economic Review, Vol. 42.

24. Conway, P., A. Drew, B. Hunt, and A. Scott(1998), "Exchange rate effects and Inflation targeting in small open economy: a stochastic analysis using FPS", BIS Conference Papers, Vol. 6. Cit. Yuong Ha, Economics Department, Bank of New Zealand-.

25. Davidson, Russell and James G. MacKinnon (1993) Estimation and Inference in Econometrics, Oxford University Press.

26. De Broeck, M., Kornelia Krajnyak, and Henri Lorie (1997), "Explaining and Forecasting the Velocity in Transition Economies, with special Reference to the Baltic's, Russia, and other countries of Former Soviet Union," IMF Working Papers/ 108 (Sept.).

27. De Soto, Jesus Huerta (2006), "*Money, Bank Credit, and Economic Cycles*," First English edition Translated from Spanish by Melinda A. Stroup, Ludwig von Mises Institute, 518 West Magnolia Avenue, Alabama.

28. Dezhbaksh, Hashem (1990) "The Inappropriate Use of Serial Correlation Tests in Dynamic Linear Models," Review of Economics and Statistics.

29. Dornbusch, R. and S. Fischer (1990), Macroeconomics, 5th ed., Economics series, McGraw-Hill International Editions (Publishing Company), New York, Printed in Singapore.

30. Dotsey, Michael (1984), "An Investigations of Cash Management Practices and Their Effects on the

Demand for Money," Federal Reserve Bank of Richmond Economic Review, 70.

31. Drew A. and B. Hunt (1998), " The Forecasting and Policy system: Stochastic simulations of the Core model", Reserve Bank of New Zealand, Discussion Paper G98/9.

32. Drew A. and B. Hunt (1999), "Efficient Simple Policy Rules and the Implications of Potential Output Uncertainty", forthcoming, Journal of Economics and Business, Special edition on Money and Monetary Policy in a Changing World.

33. Égert, B. (2001), "Estimating the Impact of the Balassa-Samuelson Effect on Inflation during the Transition: Does It matter in the Run-up to EMU?", presented at East European Transition and EU Enlargement: A Quantitative Approach, Gdansk, June.

34. Eggertsson, Gauti and Jonathan D. Ostry (2005), "Does Excess Liquidity Pose a Threat in Japan?" Policy Discussion Paper, April, Research Department, IMF, PDP/05/5.

35. Eggertsson, Gauti and Michael Woodford (2003), "The Zero Interest rates and Optimal Monetary Policy," Brookings Papers on Economic Activity, No. 1., pp.139-211.

36. Elekdag, Selim, A. Justiniano, and I. Tchakarov (2005), "An Estimated Small Open Economy Model of the Financial Accelerator," IMF Working Papers, WP/005/44.

37. Federal Reserve Bank of Philadelphia (1957): "Creeping Inflation", Business Review, August.

38. Federal Reserve System (2000), Statistics of the Reserve by the Board of Governors, a publication, March 16.

39. Fisher, Irving (1913), The Purchasing Power of Money, Macmillan, New York.

40. Friedman, M. (1953), "The Lag Effect," in the Optimum Quantity on Money and other Essays.

41. Friedman, M. (1956), "The Quantity Theory of Money: A restatement" in M. Friedman, ed. Studies in the theory of money, Vol. III.

42. Friedman, M. and A. Schwartz (1963), "A monetary History of the United States, 1876-1960" Princeton University Press, Princeton, N. J.

43. Friedman, M. and A. Schwartz (1970), "Monetary Statistics of United States", National Bureau of Economic Research, New York

44. Guillermo A. Calvo and Carlos A. Végh (December, 1990), "Money Supply and Interest Rate Policy in a New-Keynesian Framework 1," Research Department, IMF Working Paper, 119

45. Hörngren, Lars (1985), "Regulatory Monetary Policy and Uncontrolled Financial Intermediaries", Journal of Money, Credit, and Banking, Vol. XVII , No. 2, U. N. press, Ohio State, USA.

46. IMF, Internet Publication (2005), OCTWE/PDF, www.imf.org@google

47. IMF, Staff Country Reports (2000), the Sudan Country Report, No.00/70.

48. Izard, P., D. Laxton and Eliasson (1998), "Inflation Targets with NAIRU uncertainty and endogenous policy credibility", Paper presented at the Fourth Conference on Computational Economics, Cambridge, United Kindom.

49. Johnson, H. G. (1965): "A quantity theorists monetary history of the United States", the Economic Journal.
50. Johnston, Jack and John Enrico DiNardo (1997) Econometric Methods, 4th edition, McGraw-Hill.
51. Jones Charles I. (Sept. 2004), Growth and Ideas, A Handbook of Economic Growth, Version 2.0, Department of Economics, U.C. Berkeley and NBER.
52. Jones, Charles I. and Dean Scrimgeour (2005), The Steady-State Growth Theorem Understanding Uzawa 1961, version 2 of the Handbook, Department of Economics, U.C., Berkeley, NBER.
53. Judd, John P. and Glenn D. Taylor (1998), "Taylor's Rule and the Fed: 1970-1997," Federal Reserve Bank of San Francisco Economic Review (3).
54. Kasman, Bruce (Summer, 1992), "A Comparison of Monetary Policy Operating Procedures in Six Industrial Countries," Quarterly Review, Federal Reserve Bank of New York.
55. Kausar Hamdani and Stavros Peristiani (1991), "A Disaggregate Analysis of Discount Window Borrowing," Quarterly Review, Federal Reserve Bank of New York.
56. Keynes, J. M. (1930), "A treatise on money", Vol. I, London.
57. Larry Kotiff (1984), "The Economic Impact of Deficit Financing," IMF Staff Papers (Nov.).
58. Laxton, D., D. Rose and B. Tethlow (1994), "Monetary Policy, Uncertainty, and the Presumption of Linearity", Bank of Canada Technical Report No. 63.
59. Lecarpentier-Moyal, S. (1998), "Agrégats Monétairés: Théories et Applications," Econometrica, Paris.

60. Leigh, D. (2005), "Estimating the Implicit Inflation Target: An application to U.S. Monetary Policy", IMF Working Papers, WP/05/77.

61. Levine, R. (1997), "Financial Functions, institutions, and Growth," in Sequencing? Financial Strategies for Developing countries, ed. By Alison Harwood and Brue Smith, Brookings Institution, Washington.

62. Lloyd, B. Thomas (1997), Money, Banking, and Financial Markets, Irwin/ McGraw-Hill, Boston, U.S.A.

63. Lloyd, B. Thomas and A. Abderrezak (1988), "Anticipated Future Budgwet Deficits and the Term Structure of Interest Rates," Southren Economic Journal, July.

64. Loyd, S. J. (1841), "Declaration in the Report from the Select Committee on the Banks of Issue," British Sessional Papers, IV: 1, London.

65. Magzoub, A. Ahmed (2000), "Features of Islamic Economic Model," An Article in the Biannual Journal of the High Institute for Banking and Financial Studies, Vol.4, Khartoum.

66. Maurer, R. W. (2005), "A simple Economic Theory of Money Supply and Some Comments on Monetarist Double Count," A Discussion Paper, May, Pforzheim University of Applied Sciences, Germany.

67. McConnell, Campbell R. and Stanley L. Brue (1993), Economics: Principles, Problems, and Policies, 12th ed., McGraw-Hill Inc., New York.

68. Mohamed Khare, Osman Hammed (2000), "Islamic Policies and Mechanism for Controlling: An Evaluation of Outstanding Experiences on CMCs and GMCs," Journal of Banking and Financial Studies, No.

4, Dec., High Institute for Banking and Financial Studies (H. I. B. F. S.), Khartoum.

69. Nasur, Abdul-Mhamuod M. (1997), An Introduction to the Econometrics, 1st edition, Libraries Affairs Department, King Saud University, Riyadh, Kingdom of Saudi Arabia (in Arabic).

70. Ngatani, K. (1978), The Monetary Theory, An Advanced Textbooks in economics; 10, 2nd ed., North Holland Publishing Co. Amsterdam, New York, Oxford.

71. Osman, Abdul Wahab (2000): The Economic Reform Methodology in Sudan, an analytical study for economic developments in Sudan during the period (1970-2000), Money Coinage Center, Khartoum, Sudan (in Arabic).

72. Patinkin, D. (1965), Money, Interest and Prices, New York, Harbor and Row.

73. Pesaran, M. Hashem and Richard J. Smith (1994), "A Generalized R^2 Criterion for Regression Method Estimated by the Instrumental Variables Method," Econometrica, 62 (May).

74. Pindyck, Robert S. and Daniel L. Rubinfeld (1998) Econometric Models and Economic Forecasts, 4th edition, McGraw-Hill.

75. Piñón-Farah, M. (1998), "Demand for Money in Mozambique: Was There a Structural Break?", IMF Working Paper/98/157, African Department.

76. Press, W. H., S. A. Teukolsky, W.T. Vetterling, and B.P. Flannery (1992) Numerical Recipes in C, 2nd edition, Cambridge University Press.

77. Quandt, Richard E. (1983), "Computational Problems and Methods," Chapter 12 in Handbook of Econometrics, Volume 1, North-Holland.

78. Ramey, Valerie (1993), "How Important is the Credit Channeling the Transmission of Monetary Policy?" Carnegie-Rochester Conference Series on Public Policy, 39 (Dec.).

79. Rude Busch, G. D. and L. Sevensson (1998), "Policy Rules for Inflation Targeting ", National Bureau of Economic Research, Working Paper, 6512.

80. Saeed, Mohammed (2004), The Developing Course of the Bank of Sudan: features, distinction, and method, 1st ed., Khadir Press, Khartoum.

81. Sargent (1982), "The End of Four Big Inflations," in R.Hall (ed.) Inflation, Chicago University Press. Cit Dornbusch and Fischer (1990).

82. Schabert, Andreas (May 2005), "Money Supply and the Implementation of Interest Rate Targets", Working Paper, 483, European Central Bank.

83. Sellon, Gordon (1992) Changes in Financial Intermediation: The Role of Pension and Mutual Funds. Federal Reserve Bank of Kansas City Economic Review, 3rd quarter.

84. Sevensson, LEO (1997) Inflation Targeting in a Open economy: Strict or Flexible Inflation Targeting", Discussion Paper G97/8, Reserve Bank of New Zealand.

85. Shuetrim, G. and Thompson (1999) The Implications of Uncertainty for Monetary Policy, in Benjamin Hunt and Adrian Orr (eds.) Monetary Policy Under Uncertainty, Wellington, New Zealand.

86. Siegel, Barry N. (1982): Money Banking and Economy, A: monetarist view, An Arabic ed. 1987, Dar Elmurrikh, Riyadh, (in Arabic).

87. Silk, L. S. (1975): Contemporary Economics Principles and Issues, McGraw-Hill.

88. Simons, H. (Feb. 1936), "Rules versus Authority in monetary Policy," Journal of Political Economy.
89. Sudan now Research Unit, Sudan Year Book, 1983.
90. Taylor, J. B. (1998), "The Robustness and Efficiency of Monetary Policy Rules as Guide Lines for Interest Rate Setting at European Central Bank", Institute for International Economic Studies, Seminar Paper, 649.
91. The Bank of Sudan, Annual Report, Various Issues.
92. The World Bank (Oct.1985): "Sudan Prospects for Rehabilitation of Sudanese Economy", Sudan Main Report: A mid-Term Review of the Economic Recovery Program .
93. Tobin, J. (1983), "Macroeconomics: Prices and Quantities, Brookings Institution, Washington.
94. Woodford, M. (2003), Interest and Prices: Foundations of a Theory of Monetary Policy, Princeton: Princeton University Press.
95. Yuong Ha (2000), "Uncertainty about the Length of the Monetary Policy Transmission Lag: Implications for Monetary Policy", Discussion Papers Series, Reserve Bank of New Zealand, Dp2000/01, p.2.
96. Zakaria, Mustafa (1999), "The Ideal Money Stock In Sudan", OSSREA Nowsletter , Vol. XVII, NO. 2, Jne.
97. Zavdjil, M., S. Crean, A. Kireyev and A. Arvanitis (2000), "Sudan: Staff Report for the 2000 Article IV Consultation and Fourth Review of the First Annual Program Under the Medium-Term Staff-Monitored Program," IMF Staff Country Report, 00/70, Washington D. C.

33. Appendix

Schedule (1) : The growth rates of: Effective demand for Liquidity (lt), the General Price level Index (pt), Bank loans (blt), excess Reserves held by Banks (ert), Money supply (mt), and Trend of Real output (try)

obs	Lt	pt	Blt	ert	mt	try
1972	4.925295	0.14842	4.440178	4.142301	5.108367	72
1973	5.126876	0.29267	4.592895	4.591744	5.318267	73
1974	5.3924	0.518794	4.813971	4.660436	5.585674	74
1975	5.527721	0.722706	5.226123	4.947335	5.735023	75
1976	5.72574	0.741937	5.431055	5.349533	6.068101	76
1977	6.049191	0.900161	5.578144	12.52933	6.049191	77
1978	6.154008	1.068153	5.838401	5.70412	6.55953	78
1979	6.647455	1.358409	6.133181	5.969884	6.84216	79
1980	6.947543	1.591274	6.384958	6.400364	7.116483	80
1981	7.154107	1.793425	6.656122	6.624086	7.358582	81
1982	7.440211	2.03862	7.040992	6.960485	7.678345	82
1983	7.705429	2.309561	7.227604	7.212064	7.928226	83
1984	7.8439	2.590017	7.383486	7.13961	8.089942	84
1985	8.311413	2.970414	7.482519	7.749764	8.717371	85
1986	8.671756	3.225255	7.769632	8.024708	8.956235	86
1987	8.958391	3.448081	8.240812	8.389862	9.250272	87
1988	9.300064	3.847591	8.412914	8.594381	9.561603	88
1989	9.846854	4.401952	8.505414	9.084833	10.0305	89
1990	10.20184	4.904237	8.94469	9.492206	10.36232	90
1991	10.66505	5.713964	9.548726	9.954181	10.87229	91
1992	11.47732	6.498734	10.40752	10.90421	11.86072	92
1993	11.98549	7.197697	10.87287	11.42268	12.50092	93
1994	12.41867	7.96771	11.52016	11.95035	12.91251	94
1995	12.93963	8.492189	11.88159	12.67247	13.46718	95
1996	13.55742	9.326837	12.73518	13.12342	13.96907	96

1997	15.40483	9.709605	12.93738	13.01607	16.58631	97
1998	15.55485	9.866658	13.0686	13.59508	16.84541	98
1999	14.34386	10.0163	13.09668	13.0444	17.06557	99
2000	16.24436	10.0937	13.58262	13.51606	15.05872	100
2001	14.81397	10.14162	13.92292	13.80863	15.27926	101

Own calculations

Schedule (2) : The growth rates of: Real Money supply (rmt), Real Money Balances (rmlb), Deviations of Real output from its L. r. Trend (devyt), Real value of Quasi Money (rqmt), Local currency Depreciation (oext), and its real rates (roext).

obs	rmt	Rmlb	devyt	rqmt	oext	roext
1972	4.959947	4.776657	6.551671	-1005.68	-1.20397	-1010.2
1973	5.025597	4.834266	6.753438	-1598.43	-1.20397	-1603.2
1974	5.066881	4.872558	7.867489	-2538.15	-1.20397	-2543.2
1975	5.012317	4.805135	6.665251	-2260.94	-1.20397	-2266.2
1976	5.326164	4.983607	6.824425	-165.698	-1.20397	-171.204
1977	5.14903	5.148864	6.998354	-1713.32	-1.20397	-1719.2
1978	5.491377	5.278535	7.013637	-1827.09	-0.91629	-1832.92
1979	5.483751	5.289046	6.875038	-3385.89	-0.69315	-3391.69
1980	5.525209	5.356298	6.798063	-2603.75	-0.69315	-2609.69
1981	5.565158	5.360487	6.860236	-2250.33	-0.10536	-2256.11
1982	5.639725	5.401592	6.910491	-2762.87	-1.20397	-2770.2
1983	5.618665	5.34978	6.856545	-3106.52	-1.20397	-3114.2
1984	5.499925	5.253879	6.683981	-3238.43	0.916291	-3244.08
1985	5.746957	5.412939	6.62979	-4625.42	0.916291	-4632.08
1986	5.730979	5.445472	6.605664	-2896.44	0.916291	-2903.08
1987	5.802191	5.510369	7.036385	-2490.12	1.504077	-2496.5

1988	5.714012	5.477684	7.387887	-4906	1.504077	-4912.5
1989	5.628547	5.444902	7.044833	-7399.75	1.504077	-7406.5
1990	5.458086	5.297609	7.189169	-6729.55	1.504077	-6736.5
1991	5.158322	4.934445	7.118747	-12242.8	2.70805	-12249.3
1992	5.361989	4.606249	7.089075	-11913.3	4.60517	-11919.4
1993	5.303219	4.787788	7.105914	-10106.4	5.370638	-10112.6
1994	4.944803	4.450963	6.842053	-11581	5.752573	-11587.2
1995	4.974992	3.402592	6.623688	-6884.42	6.729824	-6890.27
1996	4.642235	4.230589	6.700957	-13031.1	7.286192	-13036.7
1997	6.876703	4.122261	6.774108	-4703.43	7.445418	-4711.55
1998	6.978751	4.217818	6.840724	-1687.46	7.770645	-1693.23
1999	7.049272	4.327565	6.902564	-1602.31	7.824046	-1608.18
2000	4.965019	4.574469	7.027803	-788.07	7.863267	-794.137
2001	5.137641	4.933101	7.11567	-477.709	7.889834	-484.11

Own calculations

Schedule (3): The growth rates of: Rate of Inflation (inft), the Cost of Resources adjustment (dml), its Real value (rdml), Aggregate Demand (adt), Money Velocity (vt), and Budget Deficit (bdt).

obs	inft	dml	rdml	adt	vt	bdt
1972	1009	-0.33171	-1009.33	6.724673	1.689574	0.727549
1973	1602	-0.484	-1602.48	7.036061	1.809587	1.05779
1974	2542	-0.71312	-2542.71	7.229621	2.828555	1.121678
1975	2265	-0.92989	-2265.93	7.415657	1.74422	2.358965
1976	170	-1.08449	-171.084	7.653874	1.577631	2.272126
1977	1718	-0.90033	-1718.9	7.862921	1.917292	-0.19845
1978	1832	-1.28099	-1833.28	8.008864	1.590071	2.282382
1979	3391	-1.55311	-3392.55	8.183956	1.469754	3.100092
1980	2609	-1.76019	-2610.76	8.400659	1.358366	4.48526
1981	2256	-1.9981	-2258	8.735686	1.376605	2.833213
1982	2769	-2.27675	-2771.28	9.036998	1.34937	3.034953

1983	3113	-2.57845	-3115.58	9.231603	1.321633	3.793239
1984	3245	-2.83606	-3247.84	9.51502	1.283961	4.136765
1985	4633	-3.30443	-4636.3	9.787139	0.989207	4.222445
1986	2904	-3.51076	-2907.51	10.40933	0.984731	5.061328
1987	2498	-3.7399	-2501.74	10.6564	1.307907	5.428907
1988	4914	-4.08392	-4918.08	11.24655	1.726891	4.9523
1989	7408	-4.5856	-7412.59	11.52999	1.491021	5.378052
1990	6738	-5.06471	-6743.06	12.09143	1.7968	6.186414
1991	12252	-5.93784	-12257.9	12.87725	2.031526	5.303305
1992	11924	-7.25447	-11931.3	13.69521	1.801027	7.804251
1993	10118	-7.71313	-10125.7	14.36766	1.876207	7.411556
1994	11593	-8.46155	-11601.5	15.44819	1.992908	9.303102
1995	6897	-10.0646	-6907.06	16.07462	1.767554	8.368693
1996	13044	-9.73848	-13053.7	16.55425	2.170312	9.805158
1997	4719	-12.464	-4731.46	16.86781	0.002548	8.987197
1998	1701	-12.6276	-1713.63	16.13779	-0.03837	9.093807
1999	1616	-12.738	-1628.74	16.66842	-0.05184	9.093807
2000	802	-10.4842	-812.484	22.28476	2.147757	9.392662
2001	492	-10.3462	-502.346	24.3667	2.056877	10.01682

Own calculations

Schedule (4): The growth rates of: GDP (gdpt), the Capital stock (kt), the Private Investment (ivt), the Private Savings (st), Disturbance Term (u), and the volume of Reserve requirements at Banks (rr).

obs	gdpt	kt	ivt	st	u	rr
1972	6.79794	5.207003	4.655863	3.992681	71.76282	21.08
1973	7.127854	5.351997	5.435031	4.637637	88.60957	1.9
1974	8.41423	5.806635	5.57973	-2.07944	113.6425	29704

1975	7.479243	5.906564	6.057954	4.559126	122.3403	27.51
1976	7.645732	6.266245	5.990714	2.66026	146.0895	-0.06
1977	7.966483	6.213179	6.025141	-4.483	190.3226	44.78
1978	8.149602	6.240255	6.067036	4.268298	266.5749	92.78
1979	8.311914	6.273469	5.937536	-4.48864	363.5065	115.16
1980	8.474849	6.171752	5.486041	-5.84325	485.2943	68.06
1981	8.735188	5.841351	7.381875	5.036303	605.7611	64.63
1982	9.027715	7.426906	7.333219	6.620073	793.308	67.16
1983	9.249859	7.38145	7.394493	5.843544	1083.294	150.63
1984	9.373904	7.438717	6.541174	7.285849	1215.128	180.13
1985	9.706578	6.667549	7.784473	6.267959	1882.3	331.58
1986	9.940966	7.807964	8.461321	7.250636	2683.288	763.88
1987	10.55818	8.462973	8.876628	7.575585	3584.864	1100.55
1988	11.28849	8.870496	9.305687	8.269629	5175.798	1185.64
1989	11.52152	9.294245	9.236593	8.144853	8995.927	1936.21
1990	12.15912	9.225861	10.16157	8.449664	12853.95	3314
1991	12.90381	10.1444	11.19893	10.74533	21521.05	5260
1992	13.66175	11.17901	12.14398	11.19428	44047.23	1301.2
1993	14.37712	12.12314	12.96322	11.49324	93183.93	39159
1994	14.90542	12.94206	13.70351	12.4413	148889.7	66363.5
1995	15.23473	13.68221	13.70351	13.10115	233384	74791.6
1996	16.13938	13.68221	14.62971	13.49535	453241.1	133051.8
1997	16.58886	14.60834	14.91412	11.71111	591797.4	179783.8
1998	16.80704	14.89273	15.22178	13.28574	804409.8	181845.2
1999	17.01373	15.20038	13.00008	14.958	1059624	130449
2000	17.20647	12.9789	15.45777	15.22597	9818595	130804.5
2001	17.33614	15.43637	15.50355	15.28819	1550356	135428.4

Own calculations

Appendix 2:
The Actual Values of The Model System Variables
Schedule (5): Effective Demand for Liquidity (L), General Price level Index (P), Bank loans (BL), Excess

Reserves held by Banks (*ER), Wide Money (M2), and the Real Output (*Y).

obs	L	P	BL	*ER	M2	*Y
1972	137.73	1.16	84.79	62.9475	165.4	772.4138
1973	168.49	1.34	98.78	98.6664	204.03	930
1974	219.73	1.68	123.22	105.6822	266.58	2685
1975	251.57	2.06	186.07	140.7992	309.52	859.6602
1976	306.66	2.1	228.39	210.51	431.86	996.0476
1977	423.77	2.46	264.58	276324.2	423.77	1171.829
1978	470.6	2.91	343.23	300.1012	705.94	1189.691
1979	770.82	3.89	460.9	391.4603	936.51	1046.812
1980	1040.59	4.91	592.86	602.064	1232.11	976.11
1981	1279.35	6.01	777.53	753.0159	1569.61	1034.592
1982	1703.11	7.68	1142.52	1054.144	2161.04	1084.74
1983	2220.37	10.07	1376.92	1355.688	2774.5	1033.078
1984	2550.13	13.33	1609.19	1260.936	3261.5	883.4959
1985	4070.06	19.5	1776.71	2321.025	6108.1	842.3231
1986	5835.74	25.16	2367.6	3055.528	7756.1	825.2703
1987	7772.84	31.44	3792.62	4402.208	10407.4	1224.268
1988	10938.72	46.88	4504.87	5401.225	14208.6	1704.288
1989	18898.81	81.61	4941.45	8820.494	22708.6	1235.917
1990	26952.83	134.86	7667.07	13256	31644.6	1415.001
1991	42832.28	303.07	14026.82	21040	52695.5	1325.902
1992	96501.77	664.3	33107.67	54404.8	141594.5	1290.798
1993	160409.5	1336.35	52726.07	91371	268583.4	1312.155
1994	247378.1	2886.24	100726	154871.5	405352.9	1030.41
1995	416496	4876.53	144580	318848.4	705866	847.7159
1996	772526	11235.54	339483	500528.2	1165980	909.1841
1997	4900394	16475.09	415559	449581.9	15971370	971.8982
1998	5693578	19276.8	473830	802174.8	20695130	1033.166
1999	1696130	22388.33	487320	462501	25791800	1093.822
2000	11345870	24190.07	792240	741225.5	3466710	1227.55
2001	2714110	25377.49	1113390	993141.6	4322130	1332.108

Bank of Sudan, Annual Reports, Various Issues.

Schedule (6): Vlue of Quasi Money (QM), Local Currency Rate Of Depreciation against U.S. Dollars (OEX), the Actual Rate of Inflation (INFt), Wide Money Velocity (V2), Current Budget Deficit (BD), and Current Gross Domestic Product (GDP).

obs	QM	OEX	INFt	*V2	BD	GDP
1972	27.67	0.3	1009	5.41717	2.07	896
1973	35.55	0.3	1602	6.107925	2.88	1246.2
1974	46.85	0.3	2542	16.921	3.07	4510.8
1975	57.94	0.3	2265	5.72144	10.58	1770.9
1976	73.85	0.3	170	4.843468	9.7	2091.7
1977	108.09	0.3	1718	6.802511	0.82	2882.7
1978	135.34	0.4	1832	4.904099	9.8	3462
1979	165.69	0.5	3391	4.348165	22.2	4072.1
1980	191.52	0.5	2609	3.889831	88.7	4792.7
1981	290.26	0.9	2256	3.96143	17	6217.9
1982	457.93	0.3	2769	3.854996	20.8	8330.8
1983	654.14	0.3	3113	3.74954	44.4	10403.1
1984	711.37	2.5	3245	3.610915	62.6	11777
1985	1963.5	2.5	4633	2.689101	68.2	16425.3
1986	1926.4	2.5	2904	2.677093	157.8	20763.8
1987	2643.1	4.5	2498	3.698426	227.9	38491
1988	2990.5	4.5	4914	5.623144	141.5	79897
1989	3809.8	4.5	7408	4.44163	216.6	100863.2
1990	4691.7	4.5	6738	6.030321	486.1	190827.1
1991	9863.2	15	12252	7.625718	201	401841
1992	45092.8	100	11924	6.055864	2451	857477
1993	108173.9	215	10118	6.528695	1655	1753499
1994	157974.8	315	11593	7.336842	10972	2974010
1995	289370	837	6897	5.856511	4310	4133912
1996	393450	1460	13044	8.76102	18127	10215174

1997	5806480	1712	4719	1.002551	8000	16012110
1998	760897	2370	1701	0.962358	8900	19916126
1999	883050	2500	1616	0.949482	8900	24488851
2000	1120840	2600	802	8.565621	12000	29694524
2001	1608260	2670	492	7.821502	22400	33805550

Bank of Sudan, Annual Reports, Various Issues.

Schedule (7): Capital Stock (*K), Current Private Investment (IV), Current Private Savings (S), Disturbance Term (*U), Volume of Reserve Requirements at Banks (*RR).

obs	*K	IV	S	*U	*RR
1972	182.5462	105.2	54.2	71.76282	21.08
1973	211.0293	229.3	103.3	88.60957	1.9
1974	332.4984	265	-8	113.6425	29704
1975	367.4415	427.5	95.5	122.3403	27.51
1976	526.4965	399.7	14.3	146.0895	-0.06
1977	499.2859	413.7	-88.5	190.3226	44.78
1978	512.9891	431.4	71.4	266.5749	92.78
1979	530.3138	379	-89	363.5065	115.16
1980	479.0247	241.3	-344.9	485.2943	68.06
1981	344.244	1606.6	153.9	605.7611	64.63
1982	1680.6	1530.3	750	793.308	67.16
1983	1605.917	1627	345	1083.294	150.63
1984	1700.567	693.1	1459.5	1215.128	180.13
1985	786.4658	2403	527.4	1882.3	331.58
1986	2460.116	4728.3	1409	2683.288	763.88
1987	4736.12	7162.6	1950	3584.864	1100.55
1988	7118.812	11000.4	3903.5	5175.798	1185.64
1989	10875.25	10266	3445.6	8995.927	1936.21
1990	10156.42	25888.9	4673.5	12853.95	3314

1991	25448.11	73052.3	46413	21521.05	5260
1992	71611.65	187960	72713	44047.23	1301.2
1993	184083.3	426439	98051	93183.93	39159
1994	417506.6	894045.9	253039	148889.7	66363.5
1995	875200.2	894045.9	489506	233384	74791.6
1996	875200.2	2257378	726033.9	453241.1	133051.8
1997	2209630	3000002	121919.2	591797.4	179783.8
1998	2936510	4080689	588739	804409.8	181845.2
1999	3994286	442450	3134572	1059624	130449
2000	433178.1	5166847	4097844	9818595	130804.5
2001	5057418	5408888	4360916	1550356	135428.4

Bank of Sudan, Annual Reports, Various Issues.

Schedule (8): Total Banks Deposits (TD), Investment Deposits (DI), The (DDO), Demand Deposits (DD), and Narrow Money Supply (M1).

obs	TD	DI	*DDO	DD	M1
1972	86.29	2.36	83.93	62.51	137.7
1973	105.81	5.13	100.68	75.72	168.5
1974	141.37	5.88	135.49	100.98	219.5
1975	171.92	8.2	163.72	123.06	251.6
1976	224.68	14.17	210.51	153.85	306.6
1977	332943	22.27	332920.7	224.74	423.7
1978	428.41	33.54	394.87	191.54	570.6
1979	548.08	39.69	508.39	390.69	770.82
1980	720.01	51.05	668.96	532.44	1040.62
1981	942.55	115.06	827.49	649.6	1279.1
1982	1339.56	218.13	1121.43	882.7	1703.11
1983	1781.36	275.04	1506.32	1095.87	2120.36
1984	2063.6	622.53	1441.07	1303.12	2550.12
1985	3622.63	970.03	2652.6	2124.2	4373.65
1986	5136.93	1317.52	3819.41	3069.5	5829.74

1987	7167.77	1665.01	5502.76	4148.6	7773.3
1988	8599.37	2012.51	6586.86	5616.6	11218
1989	13116.7	2360	10756.7	9658.5	18898.8
1990	18930	2360	16570	13840.3	26952.9
1991	29860	3560	26300	21169.4	42125.5
1992	94446	26440	68006	52985.2	66501.7
1993	167340	36810	130530	65869.8	160409.5
1994	234355	13110	221245	99476.1	247378.1
1995	416420	22780	393640	167865	146500
1996	677920	44340	633580	328140	772530
1997	710814	77600	633214	4315450	1016490
1998	1221120	137100	1084020	4872180	1308610
1999	1455190	862240	592950	615050	1696130
2000	1972240	1100210	872030	925050	2345870
2001	2741880	1613310	1128570	1175510	3522630

Bank of Sudan, Annual Reports, Various Issues.

Schedule (9): The Money Balances (*M1B), The The government Borrowings from Banking System (GB), Ordinary The government Revenues (OGR), the Percentage of Legal Reserves on Banks Deposits (LEG), and the Percentage of Planned The government Borrowing from Banking System (z).

obs	*M1B	GB	OGR	LEG	Z
1972	118.7069	127.19	162.3	25	10
1973	125.7463	149.97	167.3	2	10
1974	130.6548	190.98	209.5	22	10
1975	122.1359	250.01	287.8	14	10
1976	146	442.16	332	0	10
1977	172.2358	610.81	388.4	17	10
1978	196.0825	774.68	451.6	24	10

1979	198.1542	930.31	633.2	23	0
1980	211.9389	1120.4	691.8	10	0
1981	212.8286	1340.48	760.9	9	10
1982	221.7591	1214.16	926.7	6	10
1983	210.5621	1659.56	1251	10	10
1984	191.3068	3315.06	1469	12.5	0
1985	224.2897	5882.9	1455.5	12.5	0
1986	231.7067	5306.1	1486	20	0
1987	247.2424	8289.5	2010	20	0
1988	239.2918	11452.5	2742	18	0
1989	231.5746	19199.2	4017	18	10
1990	199.8584	25043.9	8324	20	10
1991	138.9959	36613.6	16398	20	10
1992	100.1079	80111.1	30517	20	10
1993	120.0355	144497.8	83586.2	30	10
1994	85.70947	177560	131193	30	25
1995	30.04185	266580	173340.6	19	25
1996	68.75771	495700	697770	21	25
1997	61.6986	593520	1085990	29	25
1998	67.88523	746450	1592000	26	25
1999	75.75956	1091470	20520000	22	25
2000	96.97657	1288910	33140000	15	25
2001	138.8092	1612320	36520000	12	25

Bank of Sudan, Annual Reports, Various Issues.

Figure 1

Tools of Monetary Policy

1. Open Market Operations
2. Discretionary Policy
3. Reserve requirement Policy

Short-Range Objectives or Operating Targets

Bank Reserves and Monetary Base Measures

1. Bank Reserves (R)
2. Monetary Base (B)
3. Non-borrowed Reserves (R-A)
4. Non-borrowed Base (B-A)
5. Discount and Advances (A)
6. Net Free Reserves (NFR)

Money Market yield : (Nominal or Real)

1. Federal Funds Rate
2. Treasury Bill Rate
3. Commercial Paper Rate
4. Bankers' acceptance rate

Intermediate-Range Objectives or Targets

Monetary Aggrgates

1. M1
2. M2, M3
3. Domestic non-financial debt
4. Bank credit

Long-term Interest Rates (Nominal or Real)

1. Government Bond Yield
2. Corporate Bond Yield
3. Mortagage rates
4. Municipal bond yield

Final Goals of Federal Reserve Policy

1. Price Level stability
2. High employment level
3. Exchange rate stability
4. Long-term economic growth

Figure 2

Figure 2
**Banking System in Sudan
in the beginnings of 1990s**

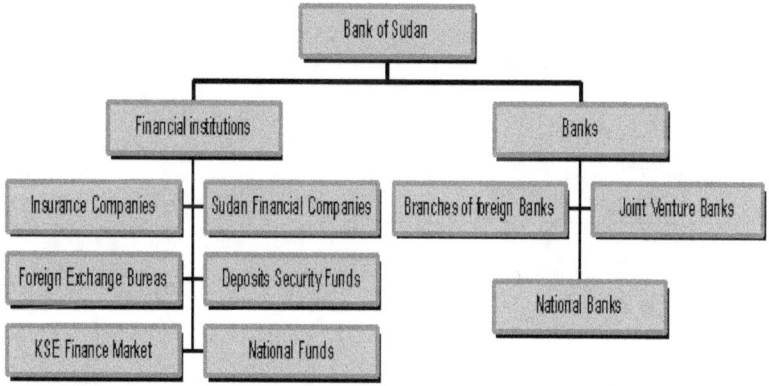

Source: the Bank of Sudan

Diagram 1   Diagram 2

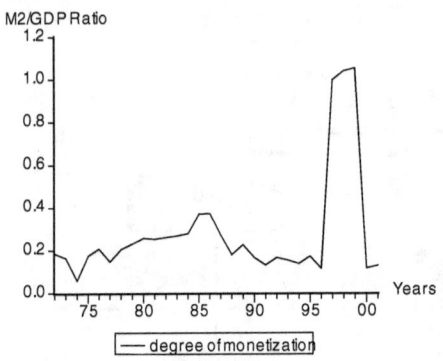

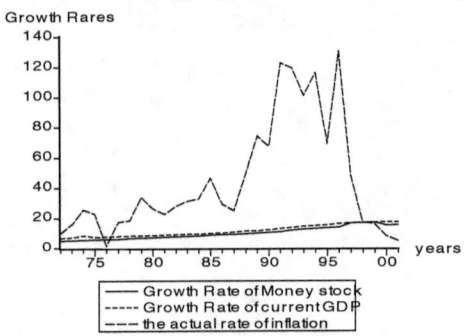

Diagram 3

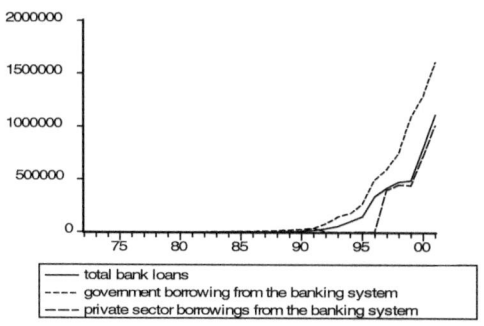

total bank loans
government borrowing from the banking system
private sector borrowings from the banking system

Diagram 4

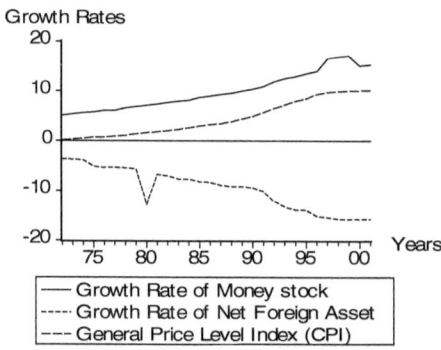

Growth Rates

Years

Growth Rate of Money stock
Growth Rate of Net Foreign Asset
General Price Level Index (CPI)

Diagram 5   Diagram 6

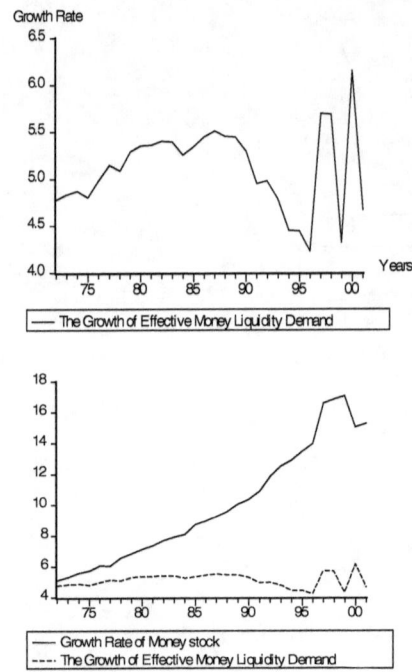

Diagram 7   Diagram 8

Monetary Economics and the Performance of the Banking Sector in Sudan

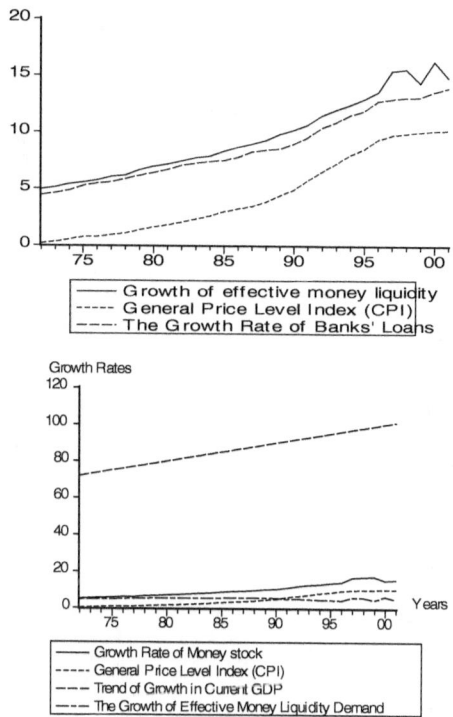

Diagram 9   Diagram 10

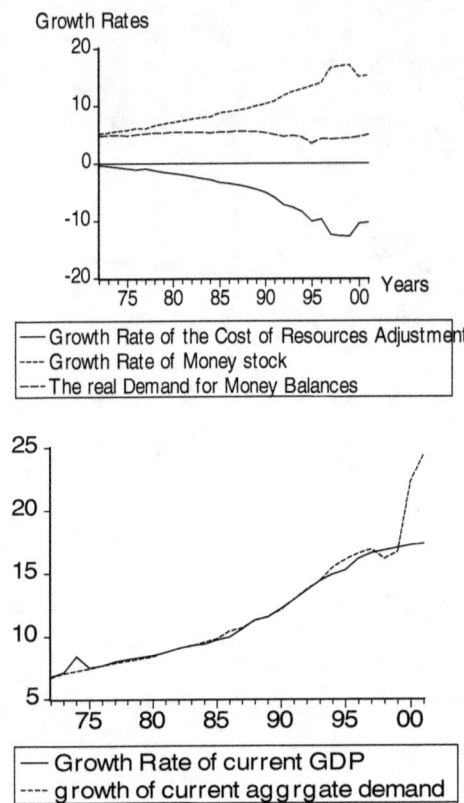

Diagram 11

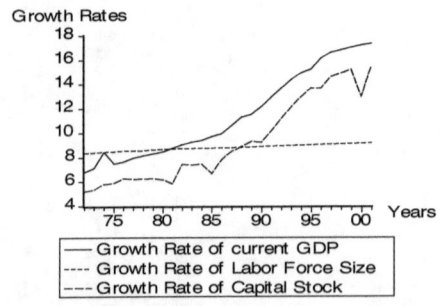

Diagram 12

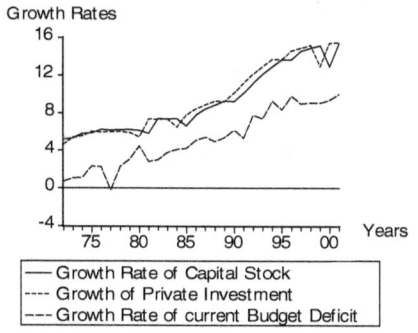

Diagram 13

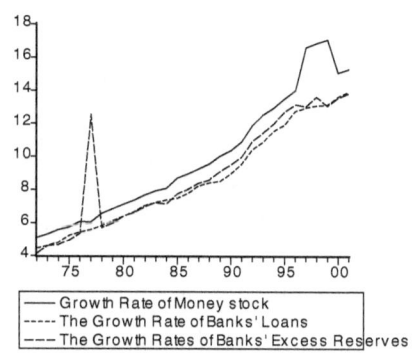

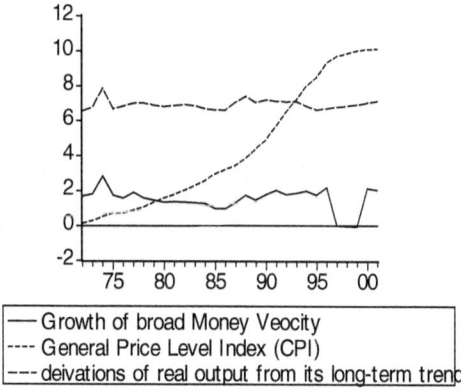

Diagram 14

The Model Equations

$$l_t = \xi_1 p_t + \xi_2 bl_t, \qquad\qquad \xi_1 > 0, \; 1 > \xi_2 > 0 \qquad (1)$$

$$m_t = m_0 + \alpha y_t + (1-\alpha) l_t + \rho H_t + e_t, \qquad H \geq 0, 0 < \alpha < 1, \rho > 0 \quad (2)$$

$$rmb_t = \beta_0 + \beta_1 devy_t + \beta_2 rqm_t + \beta_{31} roex_t^e, \qquad \beta_0 \, \beta_1, \beta_2 > 0, \beta_{31} < 0 \quad (3)$$

$$dm_t = \gamma_0 + \gamma_1 (dfm)_t, \qquad\qquad \gamma_0 > 0, \gamma_1 > 0 \qquad (4)$$

$$ad_t = \delta_1 ad_{t-1} + \delta_2 dm_t + \delta_3 v_{2t} + \delta_4 bd_t, \qquad \delta_1, \delta_2, \delta_3, \delta_4 > 0 \qquad (5)$$

$$y_t = A + (1-\varepsilon) n_t + \varepsilon k_t, \qquad\qquad \varepsilon > 0 \qquad\qquad (6)$$

$$k_t = \varphi_1 iv_t + \varphi_2 bd_t, \qquad\qquad \varphi_1 > 0, \; \varphi_2 < 0 \qquad (7)$$

$$iv_t = \omega_{11} P_t + \omega_{12} S_t + \omega_2 devy_t, \qquad \omega_{11} > 0, \omega_{12} > 0 \, \omega_2 > 0 \qquad (8)$$

$$inf_t = \lambda_1 ad_{t-1} + \lambda_2 rqm_t + \lambda_3 el_t + \lambda_4 roex_t + e_t \quad \lambda_2, < 0 \, \lambda_1, \lambda_3, \lambda_4 > 0 \quad (9)$$

$$bl_t = \theta_0 + \theta_1 er_t + \theta_2 bd_t + \theta_3 rmb_t \qquad\qquad \theta_0, \theta_1, \theta_2, \theta_3 > 0 \quad (10)$$

$$v_{2t} = \pi_0 + \pi_1 pt + \pi_2 devy_t + \pi_3 rm_t + \pi_4 bd_t, \qquad\qquad (11)$$
$$\pi_0, \pi_3, < 0, \pi_1, \pi_2, \pi_4 > 0$$

$$bd_t = \psi_1 bl_t + \psi_2 devy_t + \psi_3 inf_t, \qquad\qquad \psi_1, \psi_3 > 0, \psi_2 < 0 \quad (12)$$

Note:

The lower case letter indicates the logarithm of a variable (e.g., mt = log Mt) except the inflation (inft) and depreciation (oext) rates its actual figures are used. (see the notations for interpretation of the variables and parameters symbols).

The Model specification

The endogenous variables are:

1- Growth of real effective liquidity, it is a function of Price level and Bank loans.

2- Growth of broad money supply, it is a function of Price level, The trend of real output, and effective liquidity of money.

3- Growth of real broad money balances or $(M2)^d$, it is a function of deviation of real output from its trend, real quasi money, real depreciation of local currency, the actual rate of inflation.

4- Growth of cost of resources adjustment, it is a function of the difference between growth of real money balances and its stock.

5- Growth of aggregate demand, it is a function of its first lag, real cost of resources adjustment, wide money velocity, and the current budget deficit.

6- Growth of real output, it is a function of Labor force size and the capital stock.

7- Growth of capital stock, it is a function of private investment, and budget deficit.

8- Growth of private investment, it is a function of Price level, private savings, the deviations of real output from its trend.

9- The actual rate of inflation, it is a function of first lag of aggregate demand, real quasi money, effective demand for liquidity, and the depreciation in value of local currency.

10- Growth of banks' loans, it is a function of excess reserves at Banks, current budget deficit, and effective demand for liquidity.

11- Growth of wide money velocity, it is a function of the Price level, deviations of the real output from its trend, and the real growth of wide money.

12- Growth of budget deficit, it is a function of Bank loans, deviations of real output from its trend, and the actual rate of inflation.

ABOUT THE AUTHOR

Insert author bio text here. Insert author bio text here

www.ingramcontent.com/pod-product-compliance
Lightning Source LLC
Chambersburg PA
CBHW051500170526
45166CB00001B/325